Unleashing Your

Inner Healer

Becoming Free Through

Hypnotherapy

AUTHOR

PARVIZ SHAFAGHI, PSY.D.

DOCTOR OF CLINICAL PSYCHOLOGY

EDITED BY

DARCY CROSMAN, ED.D.

Unleashing Your Inner Healer: Becoming Free Through Hypnotherapy

Copyright © 2013 by Parviz Shafaghi, Psy.D.

www.parvizhypnotherapy.com/

Paperback ISBN 978-0-9893323-0-9
Hardcover ISBN 978-0-9893323-1-6

Printed in the United States of America

DEDICATION

This book is dedicated to my wife, Farzaneh,

who supported me with love and passion

throughout the creation of this book.

ACKNOWLEDGMENTS

I want to thank my daughter, Mojdeh, for the joy she brings to me through her brightness, creativity, and maturity, and my son Shahin, my eagle, who opened the window to true aliveness in my life. I'd like also to thank my mother for her honesty and loyalty and my father for his encouragement and kindness.

I want to thank Darcy, my editor, for her expertise and her understanding of psychology and cross cultural studies. I thank the divine source that gave me the power to be a productive and successful citizen in the United States. And finally, thanks to the people of the United States of America and Iran for the great support I have been given throughout my project and my career.

TABLE OF CONTENTS

LETTER FROM A CLIENT

I just wanted to send you a letter of thanks for your services and what you offer the community. Words are not enough. When I first considered speaking with you, honestly, I had my hesitations and reservations. I was not sure if I could trust you or whether this would work out for me. I did not have an understanding of what hypnotherapy really was. I had heard about the conscious and subconscious mind and the importance of dealing with the real core issues that are keeping us stuck in the same habits that we have been trying to get rid of for decades. Before I met you, I had tried many times to overcome them and only wound up feeling discouraged, depressed, and hopeless about the possibility of ever being able to change these patterns. I was a good person–smart, but I could not figure it out.

The biggest revelation I had was that the changes that we are looking for occur at deeper levels. The places we find ourselves stuck and don't know why are not going to be reached and overcome through determination and discipline. Our behaviors come from "our belief systems" that are deep within our subconscious minds, which have been created through life experience. These beliefs cause us to interpret life in a certain light. I came from an environment that was degrading, cruel, abusive, controlling, and much more. And that created in me a sense of unworthiness, lack of confidence, anger, etc. My way of coping with all these feelings was food. Since I have been to your practice I have lost 20 pounds, and I feel so much happier; I do not react in anger, nor am I short tempered anymore; I am more relaxed, think clearer, and feel more centered. It is kind of like when you need to go to the chiropractor and you get adjusted, and wow, you feel good and the pain goes away. That is what it's like here. You feel so much better and the pain goes away.

What relief! What freedom from not having to try and try with all that I had in me. On my own, my efforts kept failing; I tried hard to quit compulsively eating. I found out that it was what was stored in my subconscious mind that was driving my behavior. When you want to quit something, or want to do something, but you have internal brakes or can't get unstuck, that is the subconscious mind at work. That is exactly what Dr. Shafaghi addresses with hypnotherapy. These behaviors did not make me a bad person; it was just my silent cry of desperation and my way of coping with my pain that made me behave the way I did.

I have now accepted the things about myself that I had rejected; I love and appreciate who God made me to be, and I am not cruel to myself anymore. I was my worst enemy. I didn't need any enemies; I abused myself with the things I believed and said to myself day in and day out. When someone has abused you, you do not feel worthy of love, kindness, or any other good things life has to offer. It is hard to accept compliments because the picture we have of ourselves rejects the heartfelt kind words others say. We want to accept them, but we don't know how. We don't absorb them, and what makes it even worse is that we so desperately want to.

I was in such a sad space. I was married to a wonderful husband for 17 years and could not take in the love and compliments he tried to give me. I was in an internal prison. I wanted to get out but did not know how. That, right there, is the subconscious at work, and that is where the hypnotherapy took over and accomplished what I had tried to do for years in therapy and counseling; it took care of those issues in a number of sessions. Normal therapy has its place, but there comes a point when intellectualizing things that are deeply rooted only takes you so far.

There were some things that I was able to clear up immediately, and others took more time. All in all, it was so worth it. I would do it 10 times over to feel the way I do today. I am forever changed. I feel good on the inside with love, acceptance, peace, joy, and personal freedom. The trying and trying and failing and failing is over. Thank you again.

Words cannot express my gratitude. There is no price tag you can put on internal freedom to be who you really are and love who you are. Everything changes for the better because everything is connected. I am so glad I faced my fears and hesitations and did not let them stop me. I hope that other people contemplating doing this will give themselves the chance to experience becoming free from the things that have kept them stuck. You are so worth it. Life doesn't have to feel like a heavy load you are carrying on your back. This is a safe place with Dr. Shafaghi and Mrs. Shafaghi. Don't second-guess it. Do it! You deserve the freedom that was intended for you to experience. I promise you, this is an experience of a lifetime.

R. P. Butterfly

I included R. P. Butterfly's letter because I think it captures the journey so many of my clients go through, which I am attempting to describe in this book. R. P. Butterfly was able to get at the core of her distress and address it through hypnotherapy. I believe wholeheartedly that no matter what method you use, you must get at the core of your pain in order to heal. Her story is not unique, as you will see.

PREFACE

The intention of this book was to create a guide for people who want to learn about hypnotherapy and how it has been useful in activating self-healing and growth. For those who are interested in pursuing hypnotherapy, the knowledge this book imparts can be used to supplement your healing journey. The germinating idea was to create a book that would educate anyone who might benefit from these techniques by making the journey less mysterious. I think that the theory, groundwork, and techniques you will learn will give you a sense of safety and confidence in this tool for healing. A hypnotherapist, moreover a hypnoanalyst, can then help you unleash your own unique, self-healing potential and give you techniques you can use to further this healing on your own.

THE STORY OF THE MERCHANT AND HIS PARROT (A SUFI PARABLE) BY RUMI

Once upon a time, there was a Persian merchant, who owned a parrot. He kept his beautiful spiritual parrot in a cage. This story takes place during the time of year when the merchant made his usual business trip to India. The merchant, out of kindness, called to his staff, both maids and butlers.

"Hurry up! Hurry up . . . Come here! I am going to India for business–what shall I bring back to each of you as a souvenir?"

Each asked him for something special that they had long desired. The generous, caring merchant gave his promise to all to get them what they asked for. Just before his departure, he remembered his beautiful parrot. He asked the parrot,

"What gift may I bring back to you from the land of India?" The parrot responded,

You will see many beautiful parrots there in a large group that are just like me. They are my beloved flock, my family. When you see them, tell them about my circumstance, my situation here. Tell them how I am doing. Tell them that I have a desire to see them, and tell them that I am in your custody, in a cage, by the mandate of the heavens. Tell them that I am sending them greetings of peace. I am seeking out their guidance. Tell them that I asked, "Is it right that I am confined in this cage to die gradually, to give up my life here and perish in separation from you, unhappy, and in desperation?" And tell them I asked, "'Is it right that I stay in such severe oppression while you are able to go to and fro on the green grass and the trees?" Ask them, "Is right that I live in prison while you live in a rose garden?"

The merchant accepted the parrot's message, agreeing to deliver it to her kind. When the merchant went to the more remote side of India, he saw some parrots in the wilderness. The merchant stopped his camel and his caravan, and then, in a loud voice, he roared to the parrots and delivered the entire message that his parrot had given him in trust. Upon hearing this message, one parrot trembled greatly, fell down on the ground, and died. The merchant became sad; he was upset at the prospect of delivering this news to his parrot. He blamed himself for the death of the parrot, saying, "I destroyed the bird." He wondered, "Perhaps she was a relative of my little parrot? Or, perhaps they were of two bodies and one spirit? Why did I do this? Why did I deliver this message and burn up the helpless species by this vulgar speech?" The merchant continued feeling sad after he completed his business and returned home. The merchant had gifts for entire household: all the members and each of his employees. He ignored the parrot as though he had nothing for her; he felt embarrassed and humbled. But the parrot, pointing to herself, asked him,

"Where is *this* slave's gift? Tell me what you saw and whether you delivered my message!"

The merchant responded softly, "Sorry, I will tell you later."

"Tell me now," the parrot insisted. "What happened when you told my story to the Indian parrots?"

"I'm afraid to say," he replied.

"But Master, you must!" said the parrot.

The merchant was chewing on his hands and biting his fingers over what he experienced in India after delivering the message of his parrot's situation. Finally, he replied, "Why did I foolishly bring such a crude message out of ignorance and thoughtlessness?"

The parrot said, "Master, why are you so regretful? What is it that you are blaming yourself for? What is the cause of your anger and sorrow?"

"I told your grievances to a group of your beloved parrots." replied the merchant. "One of the parrots, her heart broken when she heard of your story and of your pain, trembled and died." He paused for a moment looking at the parrot, his face filled with anguish. Then he continued, " I became regretful and wondered, 'What was the purpose of my saying all that?' But since I had already spoken, what is the point of feeling guilty?"

When the merchant's parrot heard about what the other parrot did, she too trembled, fell, and became cold. When the master saw her lying still in the cage, he jumped up and threw his cap on the ground. He tore at his robe and grieved.

"Oh my beautiful, sweet-voiced parrot, what happened to you? Oh what sorrow! My sweet-sounding bird! Oh what misery! My close companion and confidant! My sweet-singing bird! The wine of my spirit, my garden, and my sweet sage! My soul is mournful because of you!"

The merchant, full of heartache, kept saying a hundred scattered and disturbed things such as these. After that, the merchant threw the parrot out of the cage. The little parrot flew to the highest branch of a nearby tree. The dead parrot made such a swift flight, it resembled the sun when it charges forth into the sky, rising up at dawn. The merchant became confused by the bird's action. All of a sudden, still without understanding, he saw that there were secrets this bird must know. He raised his head and said to her,

"Oh nightingale, share a portion of your wisdom with us in explanation. What did that parrot do so that you learned something, prepared a trick, and burned us with sorrow?"

The parrot answered, "She gave me advice by her very action."

"Meaning"–the merchant ventured.

"Meaning escape from attachment . . . because 'your charming voice is keeping you in chains.' She herself acted dead for the sake of sending me this advice."

"Meaning"–repeated the merchant.

"Oh, you who have become a singer to both commoners and the elite: become 'dead' like me so that you may find freedom!"

The parrot gave him one or two more bits of advice, which were full of spiritual insight. After that, the merchant bade her farewell.

"Go in the protection of your divine source," he told her. "You have now shown me a new path."

This is my translation and adaptation of the "Story of a Merchant and his Parrot" by Rumi, the 13th-century Persian poet. In Rumi's story, the parrot's "charming, beautiful voice" symbolizes the part of the parrot whose only role in the household was to please others. The parrot was a talking parrot who was put in a cage to entertain others.

This is familiar to many of us who sometimes feel trapped in conditions that do not allow us to be fully ourselves. Many of us work in a place we do not like; we are there because we want to please others and have a hard time leaving to do something we truly enjoy. We find it difficult to follow our bliss. The meaning of this story to me is "die before you die." We all need to let go of something we have clung to but which does not help us to truly live. It implies giving up what you think you want or need. It shows that when you are willing to let go, you can find yourself. The bird also asked for guidance from others who knew how to help her.

In this book I will show you how you can unleash your inner healer to find the obstacles that keep you from experiencing true, personal, emotional, and spiritual liberation. These obstacles restrain us from being free to be ourselves and live the life we want to live. These obstacles are often thoughts that stem from old wounds. Such wounding can create a web of false realities in our minds and in our lives. We must first identify these obstacles and their source before we are able to let go of them. In this parable, the bird discovered it was her own charming voice that kept her encaged. Through guidance, you can discover what keeps you from being free and release it.

CHAPTER 1

INTRODUCTION

*In existence, the smallest blade of grass has
the same significance and the same beauty
as the greatest star. There is no hierarchy.
There is nobody higher, nobody lower.*

Shree Rajneesh

Many people have conditions that cause them to suffer and that essentially reduce their enjoyment in life. In today's world, remedies are often believed to be outside of ourselves. We often look for solutions to our problems from over-the-counter medication. For insomnia, for example, many medications are on the market, but they seldom work because the body learns to tolerate them, or they have side effects, one of which is the risk of becoming addicted. We may also try to distract ourselves from our problems and emotions with food, movies, or overworking. However, few people are aware of the power of their own mind to heal and reduce their pain and suffering.

The aim of this book is to illustrate and support you to get in touch with your own inner power to heal. Specifically, the unconscious mind can be a powerful source of healing if one learns how to work with it. The key to unleashing this powerful healing source begins with an understanding of not only the unconscious mind but also the structure of the mind, which includes the conscious, preconscious, and unconscious mind. By understanding the way your mind operates, and by working with the aid of a hypnotherapist or hypnoanalyst, you can begin a journey that will lead to healing, self-empowerment, and self-actualization.

In this book, you will learn how hypnotherapy can help you find what is blocking you from achieving a state of happiness and how you can use self-hypnosis after therapy to continue on your healing, transformational journey. When individuals enter a state of hypnosis, they enter a period where they slow down and "take a break," in the words of Ernest Rossi, a psychologist. The brain functions on cycles of 90 minutes, at the end of which it is natural for it to slow down to this resting state. During this period of time, Rossi suggests, "People appear to be experiencing a quiet moment of inner reflection for a few minutes, where the body becomes less active, eye blinking is reduced, and the heartbeat and respiration slow down" (Fricker & Butler, p. 212). Rossi defined this state as "similar to a natural form of hypnosis" (Fricker & Butler, p. 212).

Hypnotherapy and hypnoanalysis have roots in psychoanalysis. Psychoanalysis was conceived of by Sigmund

Freud, who was the first to grasp the healing potential of the unconscious mind. He began using hypnosis and eventually developed the technique of free association to put the mind in a state of receptivity that would allow access to the unconscious. Hyponotherapy and hypnoanalysis work in a manner similar to psychoanalysis, but many professionals who use both claim that hypnotherapy and hypnoanalysis work much faster.

In this book, you will learn how hypnosis is effective at tapping into the unconscious mind to get at the root of your suffering, which will allow you to heal and transform. The unconscious mind is a source of power because it knows the areas where you began to lose faith in yourself. In the state of hypnosis, suggestions can be made to the unconscious to act on a reaffirmation of belief in one's own power.

Through hypnosis, I have successfully helped many people overcome obesity, depression, insomnia, anxiety, and tobacco, drug (legal and illegal), and alcohol addiction. Many people suffering from chronic pain have also found relief through their work with me, after having tried many other paths. This way has proven to be effective, and all that is required on your part is to accept and have faith that this process works; it can unleash your inner healer through accessing your unconscious mind.

The effectiveness of this approach is very simple. The first requirement is to accept that you have the power within you to heal. The second step is to quiet your mind. Quieting your mind is done through hypnosis with the help of a hypnotherapist, and you will also learn techniques that will help you to do this yourself. This will reduce the chatter that continually goes on and allow a deeper, reflective state of mind.

You must also admit to yourself that you have a problem that needs resolving. You must identify the symptoms you wish to remove. This path also involves an honest commitment to healing, to changing, which is often not as easy as it sounds.

In the following chapters, I will introduce you to the structure of the mind and explain how accessing the unconscious can help you overcome deep-rooted problems and be more successful in life. Once you have identified the source of your issue, techniques can be used to help reprogram your unconscious mind. In the succeeding chapters, I will cover specific ways this approach can heal problems, such as anxiety, trauma, depression, addiction, and obesity, using examples from people I have worked with who were able to overcome these issues.

Please note that the cases that illustrate the healing potential of hypnoanalysis have been disguised in order to protect the anonymity of the clients. For the most part, dialogue and quotes in these cases have been adapted by me for the purposes of this book. The exception is where clients have written about their experience; these passages are in italics.

CHAPTER 2

STRUCTURE OF THE MIND

I do not know whether I was then a man
dreaming I was a butterfly, or whether I am
a butterfly dreaming I am man.

Chuang Tse

Before you can use your unconscious mind to transform you health and relationships, it is necessary to understand the structure of your mind and the way it works. According to Freud's topographical model of the mind, there are three distinct parts of the mind: the conscious, the preconscious, and the unconscious. The conscious mind is the part that we know best. It is logical, able to reason, and can make choices. We call this part of the mind the ego. Information that comes to the conscious mind comes through the five senses.

Freud drew a sharp distinction between the preconscious and unconscious mind. He believed that thoughts that can be readily accessed are in the preconscious part of our mind. The preconscious mind helps us to retrieve immediate memories. In other words, thoughts and memories may be stored in the preconscious mind, but they are much more readily available to conscious thought than the content of the unconscious mind. The unconscious mind contains many thoughts and experiences that are beyond our awareness. Here is where many memories are stored that are repressed. A repressed memory is a memory that has been long

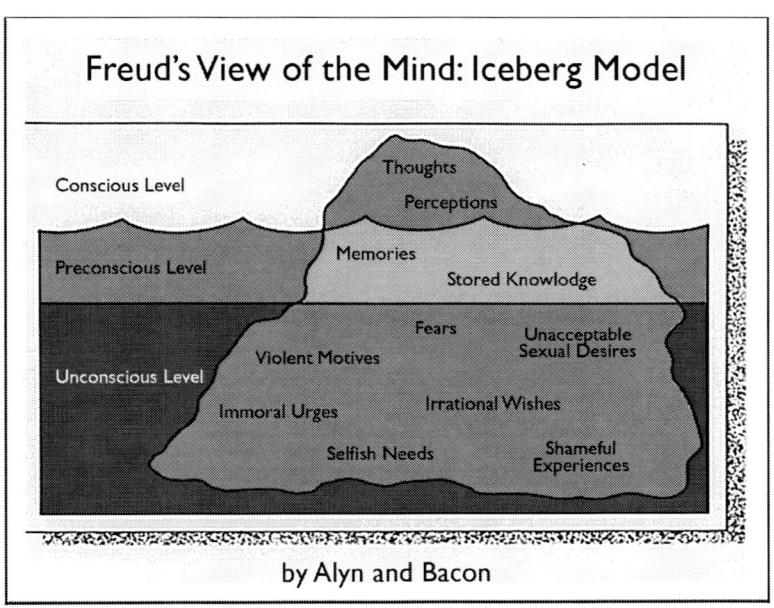

Freud's View of the Mind: Iceberg Model

Conscious Level

Thoughts

Perceptions

Preconscious Level

Memories

Stored Knowlodge

Fears

Unacceptable
Sexual Desires

Violent Motives

Unconscious Level

Immoral Urges

Irrational Wishes

Selfish Needs

Shameful
Experiences

by Alyn and Bacon

forgotten.

Our unconscious mind performs our functioning automatically and stores our experiences in a form that is not rational. According to Freud, there is "no negation, no doubt, no degrees of certainty," (p. 144) in the unconscious mind, writes Quinodoz, author of *Reading Freud*. Also, as Quinodoz noted, "The unconscious processes are timeless . . . they take no heed of reality and are exempt from mutual contradiction" (p. 144). Michael Kahn (2002) pointed out that

Freud did not discover the unconscious mind; others before him had considered its existence. However, Freud was able to describe how it worked in a way that increased the "power of therapists to help their clients and all of us to understand the nature of our own psychic life" (p. 16).

Another differentiation between our conscious and unconscious mind is in the type of thinking that predominates in each part of the mind. Secondary process thinking is typical in the conscious mind, and primary process thinking occurs in the unconscious mind. Secondary process thinking is where logic predominates, and past, present, and future are separate. In secondary process thinking, events occur in a linear fashion and are determined by cause and effect. In other words, the past and the future cannot occupy the same space. In contrast, primary process thinking operates apart from so-called reality. In the realm of the unconscious, there is no time and no recognition of past and future. The thinking goes that, "if I am suffering now, I will always suffer," and if something was hurtful many years ago, it remains hurtful and dangerous at present.

The unconscious also does not distinguish between a wish and an action. Brown and Fromm (1986) likened primary process thinking to the way a child thinks "before reality orientation and language have developed" (p. 200). Children initially live in a world where anything is possible. Primary process thinking consists for the most part in "preverbal imagery" (p. 201). Here images can represent many different ideas, and words often have multiple meanings. Primary process thinking occurs in the dream state, and it also predominates in the state of hypnosis.

In the realm of the unconscious mind, everything exists in the here and now. And this is one reason we can use it to help transform our experience now. Also, everything is taken literally in the unconscious mind. Messages told to us by our critical parents are taken as literal fact by the unconscious. Gil Boyne, author of *Transforming Therapy: A New Approach to Hypnosis,* wrote, "By age 50, the man who has been told repeatedly by his father that he 'had no guts' has had already half of his intestines removed surgically" (p. 373).

Hypnoanalysis is similar to Freud's psychoanalysis in many ways. For example, the power of suggestion is used in ways similar to the way Freud used it. Freud used interpretation to help plant a seed in the patient's unconscious. Awareness would grow around that "seed" as the patient began to respond positively to the interpretation. These seeds were specifically planted in order to help the patient become aware of the influence of the past on his or her present circumstances. Hypnotherapy and hypnoanalysis use the power of suggestion to discover the root of a problem, and, in a manner similar to the way it is used in psychoanalysis, to enlist the unconscious in the healing process.

It should be noted that Freud began his pioneering career accessing the unconscious through the use of hypnotherapy. In his writings from 1883-1888, he described how he and his mentor, Breur, treated his first patients, who were suffering from what he termed *hysteria*. Hysteria was an illness of unknown origin at the time, which manifested in physical symptoms, such as paralysis, and mental symptoms, such as hallucinations. He stated that he was able to find the cause and persistence of the symptoms and demonstrate how they could be treated through "hypnotic analysis" (Breur & Freud, 1891/2009, p. 49). Although Freud gave up using hypnosis, apparently because he never mastered the technique sufficiently well to be able to consistently bring his patients into a hypnotic state, he continued to be interested in the theory of hypnosis, especially the uses of hypnotic suggestion. He explained how with hypnotic suggestion, a doctor could simply suggest that patients stop having symptoms.

Even after discontinuing the use of hypnotherapy, Freud always gave credit to hypnosis as a therapeutic procedure for setting the foundation of his psychoanalytic work. The editor of the *Standard Edition of the Complete Psychological Works of Sigmund Freud,* James Strachey (2001), stated, "Freud never hesitated throughout his life to express his sense of gratitude to it [hypnosis as a therapeutic procedure]. 'We psycho-analysts . . . may claim to be its legitimate heirs and we do not forget how much encouragement and

17

theoretical clarification we owe to it'" (p. 68).

After his experience using hypnotherapy, Freud developed the technique of free association, in which a patient is told to say whatever comes to mind. This technique allows the unconscious to speak in its own way, through often seemingly disconnected thoughts and images, and the therapist listens without concentrating too hard on con-tent to discover its unique perspective. "With free asso-ciation, the analyst intended to create conditions in which patients could grasp the significance of their symptoms and thereby free themselves from illness" ("Sigmund Freud: Conflict and Culture," 2010).

CHAPTER 3

ROOTS OF HYPNOTHERAPY AND

HYPNOANALYSIS

It takes work to remember that we have choices. It takes discipline and a willingness to retrain our minds so that we can unlearn much of what we have learned and valued. Everything in life depends on the thoughts we choose to hold in our minds and on our willingness to change...

Gerald G. Jampolsky, MD

Sigmund Freud was one of the first to use hypnosis to uncover the traumas, or old wounds, underlying a patient's symptoms. Freud learned the technique from Josef Breur, an early mentor. In his early writings with Breur, he demonstrated in detail how "hypnotic analysis" worked to heal his patients. Many of his early patients had what was termed at the time, hysteria. In his writings of his work with Emma Von N., the first case in which he used hypnosis, he described these symptoms as "spastic interruptions amounting to a stammer" (Breur & Freud, 1891/2009, p. 49). Her fingers were clasped together and "there were frequent convulsive tic-like movements on her face" (p. 49). Although he confessed that he did not use hypnosis consistently enough with this case, the technique impressed him. He wrote that he discovered the following:

> The two symptoms were eventually linked up with so many traumas, had so much reason for being reproduced in memory, that they perpetually interrupted the patient's speech for no particular cause, in the manner of a meaningless tic.

Hypnotic analysis, however, was able to demonstrate how much meaning lay concealed behind this apparent tic; and if the Breuer procedure did not succeed in this case in getting rid of the two symptoms completely at a single blow, that was because the catharsis had extended only to the three principal traumas and not to the secondarily associated ones. (p. 93)

Catharsis is the release of emotion, which is "connected to traumatic events that had previously been repressed by bringing these events back into consciousness and reexperiencing them" (VandenBos, 2007, p. 153). Here Freud also spoke about traumas having layers. A very disturbing traumatic experience is followed by other traumas, which are connected to the first and called secondary traumas. It was Freud's belief that all of these traumas must be uncovered, and the emotions accompanying them fully processed, for healing to occur. This is also the premise underlying the hypnotherapy procedures that are outlined in this book. The passage also demonstrates Freud's success at finding the core traumas that were underlying Emma's symptoms through hypnotherapy and the success of catharsis at relieving these symptoms.

Freud also learned about hypnosis from Charcot, a renowned neurologist in 19th century France. With his reputation as a scientist, Charcot apparently legitimized hypnosis early on. It should be noted that the practice of hypnotherapy, both before and after Freud's discovery and abandonment of it, has undergone a great deal of controversy. Before Charcot "compelled the learned men of Paris to admit that hypnosis deserved recognition as a natural phenomenon and not as a manifestation of diabolical possession," wrote Kardiner (1945) in his forward to Wolfberg's *Hypnoanalysis*, "it had been necessary to reconcile hypnosis with the theological rather than the scientific conception of man" (p. ix). Indeed, Charcot was responsible for helping to make hypnosis "respectable." Kardiner added, "In the wake of this recognition, hypnosis began to flourish as a therapeutic technic [sic]" (p. ix).

Writing in 1945, Kardiner described important advances in hypnosis, notably in the interest of using hypnosis "as an adjunct to psychoanalytic therapy" (p. x); thus the term, hypnoanalysis, emerged. These "new important discoveries in exploring the unconscious" included "innovations designed to bring about specific age level regressions by means of hypnosis" (p. x). (Age regression is a key technique described in this book and will be illustrated through many case examples). Kardiner noted that these techniques not only had value for uncovering the core of an issue or trauma, but they also helped validate the theory of psychoanalysis, showing that indeed many current conflicts have at their roots some trauma embedded in the past. Kardiner also gave credit to psychoanalysis for its ability to interpret the meanings that these experiences uproot.

However, after Freud moved on to psychoanalysis, hypnotherapy again fell into disrepute by followers of Freud who may have needed to separate themselves from it in their enthusiastic embrace of psychoanalysis. Yet there were psychoanalysts who recognized its value for treating cases that were very difficult to treat by the techniques of psychoanalysis alone. The psychoanalysts who were able to effectively use hypnosis on severely troubled individuals attempted to shine a light on hypnosis as a credible treatment approach. Robert Lindner, writing in 1944, used hypnosis very successfully with prisoners, whom the psychoanalytic community had abandoned. With his own success to report, he questioned why hypnosis as a therapeutic procedure was not taken more seriously by psychoanalysts:

> Since the cavalier abandonment of cathartic hyp-
> nosis by the founding fathers of psychoanalysis
> instituted a tradition of disrepute for hypnosis
> in particular and suggestive therapy in general,
> psychiatrists and psychologists have been wary
> of identifying themselves with treatment proce-
> dures reminiscent of these methods. (p. 15)

He added that hypnosis had been disregarded without ever being properly assessed as a valid technique. He wrote, "In no place and at no time . . . has it been subjected to careful scrutiny as a respectable procedure warranting the serious and unprejudiced consideration of clinicians engaged in the study and treatment of mental or behavior disorders" (p. 15). Lindner (1944) argued that practitioners of both psychoanalysis and hypnosis had similar aims, procedures, and they both used an "interpretive core" (p. 15). He also argued, in sync with Kardiner, that hypnosis helps to validate the theory of psychoanalysis; it is another way of uncovering the unconscious concerns of patients, and it is able to demonstrate that traumatic experiences are at the root of many people's illness and suffering.

Psychoanalysts also used hypnosis with clients who had difficulty free associating. As noted before, free association was Freud's method for accessing the unconscious mind. Psychoanalysts use it today, instructing their patients to say "whatever comes into your mind." Then they listen carefully to the patterns of concern emerging from the unconscious. It is not an easy thing for most clients to free associate. We have many resistances to saying "whatever comes into our minds," even to someone we feel we can trust. There are many aspects of our experience we would simply rather not know or reveal. Often it takes years of psychoanalysis for a patient to begin to have images and thoughts, seemingly disconnected, come to mind that are the hallmark of free association. These images that emerge with free association are indications that we are swimming in the waters of primary process thinking. As a reminder, primary process thinking is thinking that is not based on reality or logic. Rather, it comes in the form of thoughts and images, where a single image can have multiple meanings. Words can have double meanings, such as in the case of puns. Primary process thinking is the language of dreams.

Another way to access primary process thinking is through hypnosis. Hypnosis helps an individual enter a state of ego-receptivity, which allows primary process thinking to predominate. Brown and Fromm (1986) wrote that patients can free associate in waking state and in hypnosis. They explained that the difference between the two is that there is a greater emphasis on imagery when one is free associating under hypnosis. They explained that a patient is able to get to the source of his or her problems much quicker with free association while under hypnosis. However, there are some patients who have resistances to free associating under any condition, even hypnosis.

Wolfberg (1985) wrote about a patient who was unable to free associate because he was suffering from schizophrenia. Wolfberg used hypnotic suggestion in order to "break through his detachment" (p. 18). He stated, though, that he proceeded with hypnosis cautiously, as he was quite concerned about what would happen if he were able to circumvent the client's strong defense against intimacy:

Hypnosis was undertaken with some trepidation, because the intimacy of the hypnotic relationship was completely opposed to Johan's character defenses and his compulsive need for isolation and independence. On the other hand, I felt that if Johan could permit himself to go into a hypnotic state, he might benefit by the experience of getting close to another person without being injured (p. 18).

Wolfberg wrote that the first few attempts at hypnosis were a failure. Johan did not respond to the hypnotic suggestion but had a nightmare that "I was sitting in a chair, and as I looked ahead of me out of the wall an opening appeared. A hand started coming toward me and I was filled with vague forebodings and a sense of horror" (p. 18). Wolfberg interpreted the dream as follows: He noted that the hand was himself, Wolfberg, reaching out to help Johan "in a therapeutic attempt, but . . . his [Johan's] need for isolation and detachment, his fear of entering into a close relationship with another person, filled him with horror and made it impossible for him to accept this help" (p. 18).

However, Wolfberg's interpretation was helpful, for Johan was then able to enter hypnosis. Johan's response to Wolfberg's interpretation shows how interpretations or suggestions that are made in the client's best interest have a positive effect. Wolfberg helped Johan overcome his resistance to being hypnotized by helping him understand the true meaning of the dream. Johan obviously had a positive reaction to the analyst's ability to speak truth to his unconscious,

for Johan was then able to trust him enough to enter hypnosis.

Wolfberg (1985) spent the initial sessions while Johan
was under hypnosis "creating a happy emotional state free
of tension, with extension of these tensionless states into
his waking life through posthypnotic suggestions" (p. 19).
Wolfberg thought that if Johan could experience pleasure
in a relationship that was close he might begin to feel less
threatened by it. Under hypnosis, Wolfberg told Johan,

> As you sit here your mind becomes occupied with
> a pleasurable scene. The most intense happiness
> comes over you. It is as though all of your cares
> are over. With each passing second you grow
> happier and happier. You recapture all of the joy-
> ous moments of your life in one. Your pleasure is
> greater than any you have ever experienced and
> it grows greater and greater. Do you notice how
> happy you feel? Now listen carefully. When you
> wake up you will continue to feel this pleasurable
> emotion, which will embrace every fiber of your

being . . . . All the unhappiness you have known will have vanished . . . Happiness will well up inside of you until it overflows, and the world will be a bountiful and joyous place" (p. 19).

After the session of hypnosis, Johan, looking befuddled but joyous, said, "It is a funny thing. . . I feel very happy, like singing. I feel like I did before I got sick, like I would like to do things" (p. 19). After this, he began to eagerly anticipate the sessions.

Hypnosis was used with Johan to overcome many of his difficulites, one of which was his lack of assertiveness. He had trouble expressing his anger at people even when he was treated wrongly, such as when someone berated him for something that had happened accidentally. Wolfberg looked for ways that hypnosis could help him become more assertive. Under hypnosis, Johan was asked to recall an event when he had stood up for himself. He felt much better after having recalled that experience. During the next session, when Johan was under hypnosis, Wolfberg suggested that upon waking up from the hypnosis he would be able to recall a dream he had forgotten. Johan then remembered a dream in which he had been late for dinner and the kitchen did not want to serve him. Yet in the dream he had insisted upon being served. He said, "I said I had been working for you [Wolfberg]. It appeared to me that I was there and that the whole incident was real. I insisted upon their giving me my food and they did. I asked them for my food and they followed through" (p. 23). These are examples of how hypnosis can be fruitfully used to help a patient access parts of himself that will help him overcome difficult issues.

Through hypnosis, Wolfberg (1985) helped Johan return to earlier states where critical events involving his mother had left him feeling impotent. That he learned something of the origins of his feelings of impotence and reaped the effects of his sessions with Wolfberg came through in a telling dream, which Johan had written in his journal:

Today I had a dream which was a picture of the transformation that my life has undergone. I saw my old life as a torn down building–waste materials and debris being carted away. I saw my new life as a newly erected structure, the building blocks of which were all kinds of odd shapes and different materials, but fitted snugly together into one unified whole. This dream is further proof to me that I have come to understand myself correctly, that I have found the pieces of the jigsaw puzzle and fitted them together in their correct positions. I have been thinking over all that has happened since the day I came under the doctor's special guidance, how everything has turned out. I have been thinking of the doctor's kindness and patience. I have been thinking of the unlimited opportunities for usefulness that lie ahead. (p. 126)

The diary shows that through hypnoanalysis Johan had come to trust and appreciate his doctor and had been able to let another human being into his world, which was also transformative.

The goal of psychoanalysis is to uncover experiences that have been buried and kept out of mind but which lie at the root of emotional illness. These experiences must emerge into the light of day and be integrated by the conscious mind for a person to heal from them. As Wolfberg (1985) wrote, "Repressed inner strivings and conflicts must be purged from the unconscious, in order that the individual may be no longer menaced by anxieties rooted in past . . . experiences and conditionings" (p. 159). Wolfberg mentioned that once the mind is free from having to spend energy with repression, "the self is enabled to proceed with the urgent task of fulfilling, in an adaptive manner, basic psychobiologic needs" (p. 159).

Wolfberg (1985) also stated that these worthy aims are difficult to accomplish because the entire being fights "vigorously against change" (p. 160). He wrote that the patient has extreme difficulty facing and accepting what is at the root of his suffering and that it takes years to uncover these issues through psychoanalysis alone. Wolfberg stated that it is the years that it takes to carry out this task that is a real downside to psychoanalysis; it is extremely expensive to be in treatment for so many years. Psychoanalysis involves both uncovering and reeducating the patient, who begins to establish new patterns to replace old ones. Both phases of treatment take years.

Wolfberg wrote that hypnosis is able to help by shortening these phases: "By cutting through interpersonal defenses, it plunges the patient immediately into a close relationship with the analyst" (p. 163). In psychoanalysis, the patient proceeds slowly, often with an unwillingness to reveal too much because he or she is dodging an intimate connection with the analyst. However, in hypnosis, the patient "experiences, from the start, feelings and attitudes of a deep-set nature, which provide material for analysis" (p. 163). Wolfberg went on to say,

> In addition to its effect on transference resistances . . . [resistance to getting close to the analyst], hypnosis has a remarkable influence on those resistances that are related to repression of traumatic memories and experiences. In a

single session the patient may bring up in a facile way memories . . . [the interpretation and integration] of which would require months of tedious psychoanalytic work. (p. 163)

A good example of how much this work can be shortened by hypnosis was given by Brown and Fromm (1986). They gave the example of a graduate student who came into therapy feeling depressed. He was unable to focus on his studies, was not interested in any activity he used to enjoy, and he wanted to leave school. The student had dreamt of a pot of peas. When asked to free associate to this dream in the waking state, this student simply said that he did not like pea soup and that all peas looked the same. When he was under hypnosis, he had a dream that he dived into a lake. The water seemed to be muddy, but as he kept going deeper the water became "clearer and clearer" (p. 204). He came to a kingdom, with a palace and a throne room, and he struggled hard to get on the throne but was unable to be successful. The student immediately perceived the meaning of his dream:

> I want to be better than everyone else. I want to
> be admired: I want to be the "king." But here at
> this university I am just one among many. We are
> all like peas in a pod. We are more or less equally
> gifted. I want to be better than everybody else. I
> am depressed because I do not get the adulation
> of my peers, as I did in high school and in the
> small college I went to. I am not "the best."

He added that he thought it was interesting that in his dream there was "a pot full of peas, in hypnosis a pod. Apparently I played with the words without knowing it" (p. 204).

Currently, hypnotherapists and hypnoanalysts help clients to discover and resolve their issues through a process similar to psychoanalysis: finding out what is in the unconscious and working through these traumatic memories. Hypnotherapy is successful because it is a relatively simple way to overcome resistance to change. There is resistance because there is fear in the unconscious mind of change, of transformation. The behavioral patterns are deeply rooted in our unconscious, and we have enormous resistance to changing those patterns. Resistance is the client's reluctance to change his or her behavior outside the therapy room. Many hypnotherapists call this resistance a "critical factor," which hypnosis is able to circumvent. As mentioned previously, psychoanalysts use free association to overcome resistance, and hypnotherapists use hypnosis.

CHAPTER 4

RESISTANCE TO CHANGE

There are only two ways to live your life:
one is as though nothing is a miracle;
the other is as though everything
is a miracle.

Albert Einstein

As mentioned before, the unconscious mind is a powerful source of healing if one knows how to work with it.
Through enlisting the aid of the conscious mind, the power
of the unconscious mind can be unleashed to bring about
healing, self-empowerment, and self-actualization. From the
previous chapter, we know that the road to healing for Freud,
the pioneer of psychoanalysis, was first hypnosis and then
free association to identify patterns in the unconscious that
are road blocks to freedom. The unconscious mind holds the
key to suffering and it also holds the key to liberation. The
unconscious has the power to dictate a person's reality, because the unconscious has been shaped by many forces and
experiences the individual has been exposed to.

From the perspective presented by Freud, the unconscious operates on our current belief systems, which are
based on our past experiences. For example, a woman that
is constantly getting involved in relationships with men who
leave her may have been disappointed in childhood by a
father who was at work most of the time and did not
even show up for her birthday. Freud's belief was that we

unconsciously repeat the same painful scenarios in order to create different, or more desirable, outcomes.

In spite of the idea that therapy or hypnosis offers relief to their suffering, clients are often resistant to change. What I mean by this is that the unconscious wields a great deal of power, and even though clients may believe on a conscious level they want to change, these patterns of the unconscious are deeply set. The resistance to change has been called the critical factor in hypnosis. Freud simply called it resistance.

Resistance is a client's reluctance to change his or her behavior, based on unconscious impulses. Resistance is partly based on the unconscious' dependence on the status quo, which has enabled the client to survive some painful past episodes. One could be fearful of the disruptions that may accompany positive change. For example, a man who wants to quit alcohol might be married to a woman who is also an alcoholic. For this man, getting healthy and forming healthier types of relationships could be threatening to the bond he has with his wife.

According to Dave Elman (1984), hypnosis sets aside

our natural resistance to change by putting us into a mind-set that allows suggestions to penetrate and make inroads into the rigid patterns of the unconscious. Brown and Fromm (1986) used the term ego-receptivity for the state of mind of someone under hypnosis. "In ego receptivity, critical judgment, strict adherence to reality orientation, and active, goal-directed thinking are held to a minimum, and the person allows himself to let unconscious and preconscious material float freely into his mind" (p. 202). They wrote, "There is an openness to experiencing, which William James (1961/1982) would have characterized as watching the stream of consciousness flow by" (p. 202).

It is this state of mind that is the predominant state in hypnosis. In a similar way that free association helps to get at a person's true concerns underneath his or her resistance, hypnosis helps to get under a person's protective defenses. When these critical factors are bypassed, the person immediately goes to the trauma.

John Lundholm (2007), also a hypnotherapist, emphasized that suspending the critical factor in no way indicates a complete suspension of critical judgment:

> In hypnosis a person suspends his or her critical factor, but not for the sake of entertainment. A person may like a positive suggestion, but unconsciously, or even consciously sometimes, constantly says, "I like it, but it's not true for me,' "I'm afraid of what will happen if I change," or "I don't really deserve to have what I want." Any positive suggestion will be rejected. Suspending the critical factor allows greater acceptance of new behaviors and thinking patterns. Just as the movie viewer never loses the ability to distinguish truth from fiction, the hypnotized person never loses the ability to reject a suggestion that is not for his or her good. That is why, contrary to popular misconception, a person cannot be made to do something against his or her will with hypnosis. (para. 5)

Lundholm (2013) believes that hypnosis actually

enhances an individual's critical thinking. Lundholm wrote, "Hypnosis is a specific learning state; it is the enhancement of critical thinking followed by selective acceptable suggestion" (para. 10). In other words, hypnosis is able to enlist a client's thinking faculties to help facilitate change. In this way the conscious mind, with the help of the techniques of hypnosis, can work to overcome prior beliefs in a way that the unconscious is more likely to accept.

As mentioned briefly, resistance to change is also reduced by the work done between hypnotherapy sessions. Much work can be done in all phases of the work, in preparing the groundwork, where an individual can cultivate a receptive mind by using techniques to quiet the mind, or through posthypnotic suggestions, which have the same aim. Also, in the working through process, after traumatic incidents are recalled, the hypnotherapist helps the client to integrate changes that help reduce the resistance to uncovering deeper, more painful memories.

Hypnoanalysis, according to Brown and Fromm (1986), is used to work through a client's problems in three phases: (a) uncovering unconscious "conflicts, memories, affects, [and] thoughts . . . against which the patient is defending himself–without piercing defenses too quickly; and (b) working through, which leads to (c) integration, mature coping, and mastery" (p. 203). Hypnotherapy also uses these three phases, although not all hypnotherapists will refer to them as such, and the duration of the working through process and integration phase may vary depending on the client's resistance and issues.

Although many people are able to get to the source of their problems quicker under hypnosis than through psychotherapy alone, they do not always go to the original trauma the first time. Many times, due to resistance, they will go to an issue that is overlaying a more significant traumatic experience. Freud called this secondary trauma. People may uncover secondary traumas first when there is deep resistance. In the following case example, the client had resistance to knowing the truth about herself, her life, and the role that other significant people played in her trauma.

Jasmine

Jasmine came in to see me because she was deeply depressed. She found no joy in her life, and she found it difficult to leave the house for any reason. When she came to the appointment, she was aware that her mind was full of unpleasant thoughts. She was aware of having negative feelings about herself and the situations in her life.

Jasmine was a housewife, in her middle 50s, married to a man that was part owner of gas station. She had two children, both adults–a 28-year old female and a 19-year old male. Both children were living out of the home. She had been laid off from her position as a teacher at a Montessori school, an alternative model for teaching children that places emphasis on children's development. She stood approximately 5 foot 6 inches tall, was a little overweight for her height, and had short dark hair framing a youthful round face, giving her the appearance of a shy young girl. Her parents had migrated to the US from the Middle East. Growing up, she had had a good relationship with her father but an argumentative one with her mother.

She said that during her childhood her mother would comb her long hair harshly, with anger. Then suddenly, her mother decided to cut it short. She said that with her hair short she resembled a tomboy and had hardly stood out from her five siblings, all of whom were boys. When I asked if she had a sister, she said her sister had drowned in the pool at their vacation house. Since the death of her sister, she did not have a good relationship with her mother. She said that although her mother had been depressed, her father had always supported her and had been a source of comfort and strength.

When she came to the appointment, she had no idea why she felt so immobilized in her life. She said, "I feel hopeless, helpless, and defeated. At times I truly hate myself. I don't know how to get in touch with my true self and what I really want." She said she had trouble asserting herself, speaking up for herself. This had occurred both at work and with her family. She said she was always careful not to make others upset, saying, "I am forever walking on eggshells around other people."

Her tendency to put the needs of others before her own

was continually backfiring on her. For example, her daughter would bring home her boyfriend's laundry and then do it in her machines. Jasmine would hold back her disapproval, but it would express itself in other ways, until she eventually burst out in anger. The daughter would leave, slamming the door behind her.

Jasmine's inability to know how to set limits, assert herself, and act on her own behalf perpetuated negative feelings about herself. She was filled with anger against herself, which manifested in negative self-talk. These negative thoughts and conflicts were getting in the way of her ability to gain a more positive, optimistic perspective on her self, her situation, and her life. Her desired state was to have more energy, feel good about herself, and to be able to concentrate.

Under hypnosis during our first session, she was asked to return to the time that these negative feelings began. She returned to a time when she was in the third grade and she was sitting with her family at the breakfast table. She relived the experience of spilling milk on the table and the way her brothers teased her mercilessly because of it. She reexperienced how humiliated her brothers made her feel. Their teasing was so relentless that she began to knock over glasses at the table almost every time they sat down to eat. The brothers continued to tease her, calling her a klutz, and she had begun to believe it herself, as she went on to repeat the behavior. The belief that she was a klutz had entered into her unconscious, and she continued to prove it to be true in other facets of life.

Reliving this incident helped her to understand how others' behavior had affected her feelings about herself. She gained a remarkable amount of information about herself from this session and uncovered many more incidents in which she had blamed herself. Specifically, she had blamed herself for her parent's conflicts.

Although she was content to have found a source for much of her self-blame, I had the sense that there was more to uncover. She, however, was not so sure. Although I was hesitant to pressure her, she decided to do another age regression. Under hypnosis, I again asked her to go to the source of the negative thoughts and feelings about herself, and this time she returned to age 5. Interestingly, previous to this session, she had not been able to revisit a time when she was younger than 8-years old, when she was in the third grade. She now said,

> I am playing in the yard by the pool, and Aisha [her sister], who is about 2-years old, is playing there too. I am playing with one of our neighbors, a boy, and my father is angry at me and telling me to go to my room. [In the culture she grew up in, families would not allow boys and girls to play together. Apparently she had disobeyed this expectation, and her father was angry with her and had sent her to her room]. I obey my father, go to my room, and continue to play on my own. [There is a pause]. I hear my mother screaming. I run into our backyard and I see my mother jump into the pool and pull Aisha out. My mother is screaming, pulling out her hair, beating herself around the head, all the while holding Aisha's dead body in her arms. I am in a corner watching,

not knowing what to say or do. The neighbors come and they do not know what to do. [A little while later] I am at the funeral. There is food. Mother's grieving has not abated.

She related this incident with the same shock and fright she experienced at the time, but when talking about it immediately afterwards, she experienced a catharsis; she cried, releasing a great deal of the pain of the incident. Watching a sibling die is one of the most traumatic experiences that can happen to a child, and that is why the memory of it–the actual experience with all of the emotions that went with it–had been buried. However, it was not the only reason the memory had been repressed. She had always known how deeply affected she had been by her mother's grief reaction. Her mother had never been the same after that. For a long time the grief had marked her. Her mother had been consumed with grief; she described her mother's look as one who had been tortured by grief. She said that she had always thought she, Jasmine, had left her sister alone, and her mother's grief seemed to be a testament to her own sense of guilt. She thought it was her fault her sister had died and that was why her mother was punishing her.

What was actually more difficult for her to realize, and what had created the strongest resistance to reliving this memory, was that it had been her father's fault all along. Her father had told her to leave. He had been so angry at her for playing with the boy that he must have forgotten for a moment that Aisha was out there. She did not know how it had happened, she could not know the circumstances that led her father to leave her sister out there alone; all she knew was that it was difficult to fathom that he could have done it. She had idolized her father; in her eyes, he could do no wrong.

After working through these memories, Jasmine began to grow her hair. She had kept it short since childhood. It may have been an unconscious reminder that she could not grow until she faced the truth about the death of her sibling. Her mother had decided to cut Jasmine's hair short, almost as if to dispense with the presence of any daughter, as though any reminder that she once had a daughter was too much.

This memory shed light on the subsequent events in her life. Deep down, this tragic incident, and the blame she heaped on herself for it, had affected her self-esteem and had manifested in many ways, with the spilling of the milk being just one example. She also realized that she had been terribly angry at her mother, which had affected her relationship with her daughter. She recognized that she needed to let her daughter have her own mind. She said, "We still have our differences; however, our relationship has improved tremendously, and she visits me much more often. I am no longer as critical of her; some dark layer of hate and anger has been lifted from me." She added, "My mind seems to perceive things differently than before."

Jasmine's true self and her true desires had long been buried far beneath the repercussions of this trauma. She was now beginning to free herself from the unconscious belief that something was fundamentally wrong with her and follow her heart to places she truly desired to go.

CHAPTER 5

PREPARING THE

GROUNDWORK

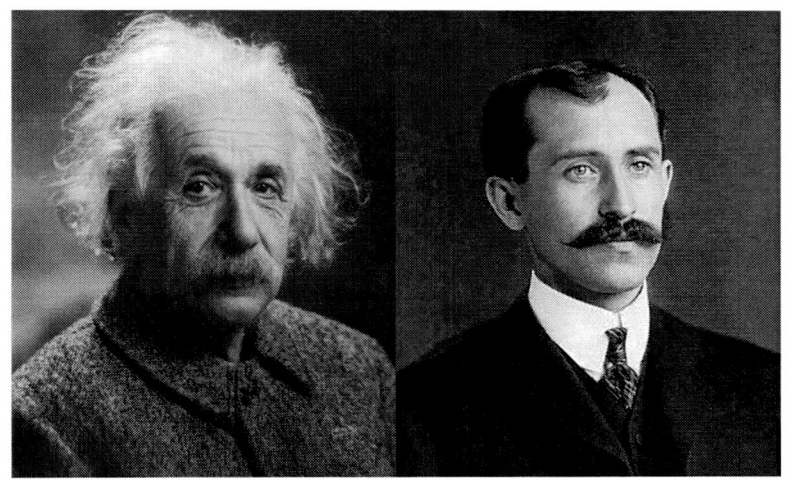

(Above: Albert Einstein and Wilbur Wright of
the Wright Brothers)

*The true perfection of man
lies not in what man has,
but in what man is.*

Oscar Wilde

In order to be truly liberated from the old ways of thinking and acting that cause us suffering, we must be ready to change. This involves making the necessary preparations for the change that we want. The first step in doing this is to recognize the problem. You must be able to identify behaviors that keep you from functioning at your optimum level. In hypnosis, problems are then traced to their root. Once they are traced to the root, they are often resolved. However, this cannot happen if you are unable to identify the problem. Elman, in *Hypnotherapy*, used the example of a an individual with a phobia who refuses to recognize it as a phobia. People may refuse to ride an escalator, he said, but they may not identify that as a phobia. A person might say, "I just don't like escalators. It isn't a phobia; it's an idiosyncrasy" (p. 182). Once the problem is recognized, there must be 100% commitment to change.

To prepare for this deep work of change, you might want to consider what life would be like once you have achieved your desired state or objective. Many times changes are hard and it is difficult to see what is standing in our way.

By thinking through what life will be like once this change has taken place, you might be able to identify all the implications, both desirable and undesirable, that might stand in your way from making this change. On the one hand, even changes you believe are positive may be threatening for some reason, such as having a fear of being successful because you might create envy in others. On the other hand, longstanding relationships might have to change. People around you may be invested in your former functioning level. Thus, your changes might threaten them and the relationship. One must deeply want this change, so much so that it becomes an overriding desire.

Another way to prepare the groundwork for change is to enlist your conscious mind in bringing about the change you desire. The conscious mind can help because the unconscious will carry out whatever messages you (and your conscious mind) give it. If you say, "I cannot afford" something that you want, then the unconscious will certainly ensure that you do not have the means to buy it. When you give your unconscious a different experience of yourself, then old patterns automatically begin to drop away.

You can prepare for this experience by immersing yourself as much as possible in positive thoughts. Techniques can be used throughout the process to assure yourself on an unconscious level that you are safe and that all the changes will reap joy in the end. There may be pain in letting go of old ways of being and relationships that are not good for us, but that pain is transitory.

When you give your unconscious a different experience of yourself, this can have a large impact, in spite of core beliefs, such as "I am not worthy, I'll never amount to anything," and patterns of behavior that carry out those beliefs. As Joseph Murphy pointed out in *The Power of Your Subconscious Mind*, the unconscious mind (also referred to as the subconscious) is constantly busy carrying out these messages, and it is important to keep the conscious mind equally busy with thoughts that are positive, loving, fulfilling, and kind to yourself. These positive thoughts send a powerful message to the unconscious. Murphy wrote, "Take care of your conscious mind knowing in your heart and soul that your subconscious mind is always expressing, reproducing, and manifesting according to your habitual thinking" (p. 42).

It is important to believe in your power to unleash the healer within you and your own potential to heal yourself. It is a living force, an intelligence, that can transform every part of your being, every cell, and every atom of your mind and body. Every cell has consciousness, and you are communicating your truth throughout your mind and body through your inner healer. All you need do is tap into your unconscious and wake your inner healer, and then let it work with you, reinforcing your commitment and power to change and to grow.

Visualization

In order to begin the process of change, you must learn how to relax your mind and body. This will help the over-busy mind reduce its activity and increase the receptivity of the unconscious mind. One way to do this is through meditation. Another way to accomplish this is through visualization. During the first interview, I teach my clients to visualize a place in which they feel comfortable. This place should be one in which you feel absolutely safe. It could be a beach, a meadow, or any place you imagine that is appealing.

Whatever you choose, you must have a great level of detail in this environment. For example, if you imagine you are on a beach, you want to use all your senses to ground yourself in that place: feel the temperature; if the sun is out, feel how warm it is on your skin. Hear the sound of the birds, smell the salt of the ocean, see and hear the waves, and feel what the sand feels like through your fingers and toes. It is also important that you are not doing anything but resting in this environment. Also, nothing should be forced. Practicing just being in this safe place will help to quiet the mind.

Autosuggestion

The reason hypnotherapy is so transformative and rapid in comparison to other modes of psychotherapy, I believe, is due to the use of techniques that make such a large impact on the unconscious mind; when used properly, they can continue to make this impact on a daily basis, even when the client is not in session with the hypnotherapist. A technique that can be used to send positive messages to yourself to counteract self-defeating messages is *autosuggestion*. With autosuggestion, you are putting thoughts associated with what you want to achieve directly into your unconscious. Joseph Murphy defined it simply as, "suggesting something definite and specific to oneself" (p. 22).

In order to utilize this tool, it is best to quiet the mind as much as possible. Center yourself in a quiet room with few distractions, and decrease the rate at which thoughts are constantly running through your mind either through meditating or using the visualization described above. In this state, you employ autosuggestion by repeating to yourself over and over the suggestion that will help you accomplish your desired goal. I will give an example of how autosuggestion was used effectively by a client I had who was afraid of dogs. Through hypnoanalysis, he traced his fear of dogs to a single incident. He remembered that at age 7, when he was crossing a street, a dog came toward him. The dog scared him, and he ran into the street and was hit by a taxi. Since then, he had a great fear of dogs. He was even afraid to walk through neighborhoods, fearing a dog would come out of a house.

After his marriage, he would hide behind his wife when they came across a dog. In order to work with his fear, he used the following autosuggestion, "It was not the dog's fault that I was hit, and dogs are generally friendly." He used this autosuggestion once a day for 40 days. The autosuggestion, along with the working through of the original incident, was enough to remove his fear of dogs. He later got a dog for himself.

Willingness

In order to successfully engage your entire self in the process of change, you must be willing to change. Willingness does not hinge on the ability to be hypnotized. In my experience, all clients are able to undergo hypnosis, even those who think they cannot. This is not only my experience, but other hypnotherapists support this contention as well. Elman (1984) noted that there was no such thing as not being hypnotizable, even though, as was observed in Wolfberg's (1945) case of Johan, one may initially resist allowing oneself to enter the hypnotic state.

Because of the intense resistance to change that accompanies dysfunction, it is unlikely that a client will be 100% committed to change. As stated before, this is because the power of the unconscious is directed towards maintaining the status quo. Therefore, therapy often consists of laying the groundwork for transformation through hypnotherapy.

Preparing the groundwork for change involves a great deal of courage and an honest appraisal of your life. There must be a willingness to clear out past conditioning that does not support new life. This will necessitate a rooting out of trauma, which is accomplished through hypnosis. For example, someone who uses drugs or alcohol may be using them as a way to numb unwanted emotions. Through hypnosis, the unconscious mind will bring to the surface the emotions one is trying to cover up and the traumatic experience underlying those. Once all of that is revealed, relief comes. It is like a tsunami; it is scary, but once it is over, everything settles, and the changes you have been seeking also become settled.

The entire process feels much safer with the support of a hypnotherapist. Together, the therapist and client shed light on what is in the unconscious mind and work at uncovering the roadblocks to health and wellness. I will now elaborate on the procedures through which they accomplish this.

CHAPTER 6

PROCESS OF CHANGE

Reasoning can never manifest the truth . . . .
Truth must be
seen

Molana-al-Moazam Hazzrat Shah Maghsoud
Sadegh Angha

from *Sayings of the Sufi Sages*

Lynn Wilcox

Orientation to hypnotherapy

During the first appointment, I orient clients to hypno-therapy. I ask what they think about hypnotherapy and whether they have experienced it in the past. I want to make sure I clear up any misconceptions about hypnotherapy they may have. Then I introduce them to the procedures of hyp-nopsis. I ask them to think of a safe place where they can utterly relax. I tell them to use as much detail as possible to feel they are in a real place. The place they envision must be utterly stress free. This is a point of safety for them that they can return to at any time during the therapeutic process.

I then conduct a thorough interview, including the creation of a genogram, which is a sort of family tree that shows the family's history: births, deaths, and traumatic his-tories, such as suicides and stillbirths. In the genogram, I also identify important relationship issues between family members. For example, there may be a pattern where family members stop talking to one another and disconnect from each other emotionally. It is good to know what intergener-ational patterns the client is dealing with.

Role of the Therapist

I do not give suggestions from my own value system; I believe wholeheartedly that change comes from the person's willingness to change. I know that change happens naturally and depends on multiple factors: a client's readiness for change, commitment to change, and unique personal situation. I also know that many people come to me only when they are ready. My role is to guide them through the process of change. As a hypnotherapist, I pay attention to the complete process of my clients and try to understand the problem from their point of view. Any hypnotic suggestion comes about through a dialogue between myself and the client. The client's wellbeing, safety, and confidentiality come first and foremost, and the therapy is conducted solely in the best interests of the client.

Problem State Versus Desired State

The core of this therapy is to identify the problem the client wants to resolve and how the person imagines his or her life will be once the problem has been resolved.

On a trip to Iran, I gave a workshop about my work. I asked for a volunteer and asked about her perceptions of, and experience with, hypnosis. Since this was for the purposes of a demonstration, I instructed her to keep to herself what her problem was and what she was experiencing under hypnosis. I told everyone that I wanted to ensure a sense of safety with the proceedings. I assured the participants that there would be no side effects. I met with her afterwards to give her a chance to debrief. I made sure that she needed no further help with integrating her experience and insights. I also gave her my business card and some resources in Iran should she need them. In order to help her relax her mind and body, I said, "I'm going to count from 10 to 1; with each successive number, your mind and body will become more relaxed, and you will go deeper and deeper into the hypnotic state."

This volunteer had no experience with hypnosis. This was her first introduction to it. She said she wanted to see how it worked. I was a little concerned that we would encounter resistance. She acted as though she didn't have any problems. One can see from the photo that she was smiling and appeared to be relatively happy. She was interacting with me in a carefree manner and telling the workshop participants that nothing was likely to happen. The others appeared to be wondering what this educated Iranian American had to teach them and expressed some skepticism. I was reminded that even today the process of hypnosis is shrouded in mystery, and people like to poke fun of things they do not understand. Someone even remarked, "You look like you are presenting a magic show." I had my Power Point presentation set up and was giving demonstrations using volunteers.

All of what clients wish to change in their lives is called the *problem state*. The *desired state* is the state they will be in when the problem is gone. To help them to clarify the problem and desired state, there is a form to fill out. Here they write in detail about the problem they would like to change. They are asked to write about how they feel physically when they are in the problem state, what they experience emotionally when they are in the problem state, and what they experience mentally in that state. Then they are asked to write in detail about what their lives will be like once they achieve their desired state.

As you read this now, you may wish to go through the exercise. Ask yourself how you feel physically, emotionally, and what your thoughts are when in the problem state. Then, ask yourself how you will feel when the problem has been resolved. How will you feel in your body? What will you be feeling emotionally once you have achieved this state? And what might you be thinking in this state? A form follows that you can use for writing down what you wish to change; it is the form I give my clients.

Model for Creating "Problem State/Desired State" Scripts

1. Problem State: Please tell me about the problem you would like to change. Write in as much detail as possible the problem and how you experience this problem.

_____

_____

_____

    • How do you feel physically in this state?

_____

    • How do you feel emotionally in this state (e.g., mad, sad, scared)?

_____

    • What do you think when you are in this state?

_____

2. Desired State: Use as much detail as possible to tell me what you will be experiencing when you have achieved your desired state. Visualize what this state is like.

_____

_____

_____

    • What does your body feel like in this state?

_____

    • What are you experiencing emotionally in this state?

_____

    • What are you thinking about in this state?

_____

Here, my volunteer is under light hypnosis. I am telling her, "Whatever is on your mind, go to its source." I thought it was important not to have her think of a particular problem in this instance because that would be assuming she had a problem. I knew she was wanting to volunteer for a reason and that there was something that she needed to resolve. I should also add that even when a client has a specific problem in mind, under hypnosis, he or she will follow something more urgent residing in the unconscious.

Induction: Mind and Body Relaxation

Before one can enter a hypnotic state, it is necessary to relax one's mind and body. I ask clients to go to the safe place they created in the beginning of the interview. This will help them enter an ego-receptive state of mind. Brown and Fromm (1986) used the term ego-receptivity for the state of mind of someone under hypnosis. They wrote, "There is an openness to experiencing. . . [to] watching the stream of consciousness flow by" (p. 202). It is this state of mind that is the predominant state in the hypnosis and self-hypnosis. During the next phase, such as an age regression, clients enter a deeper state.

Age Regression

During an age regression, clients relive past events of their lives, while in the hypnotic state. I will give plenty of examples of this in the cases throughout the book. Before undergoing an age regression, clients must enter a deeper state of hypnosis. In order to facilitate this deeper state, I tell them, "I am now going to count down from 3 to 1 and with each count you go deeper and deeper into the unconscious mind."

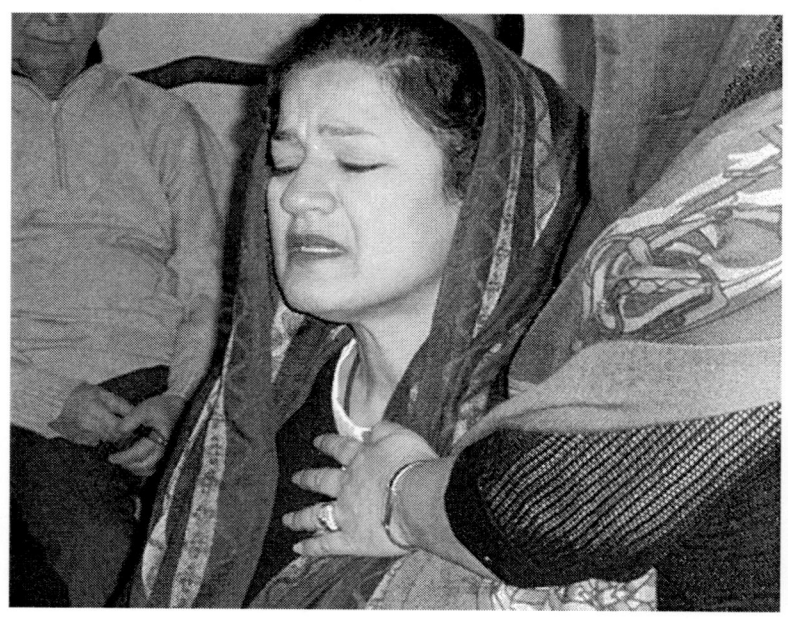

The beginning of the abreaction: The volunteer went to the source and at this point, she was starting to remember a traumatic incident that was at the root of her current problem.

During age regression, I look for signs that the client is experiencing something important. These cues might consist of body tension, changes in breathing, rapid eye movements, and facial expressions. When I notice these cues, I ask them to tell me where they are and what is happening.

Becoming conscious of repressed experiences: Here the volunteer is reliving the traumatic experience that was at the source of her problem. She is releasing the pain that she had been carrying for many, many years.

Becoming Conscious of Repressed Experiences

Reliving traumatic experience that is uncovered during age regression is called *abreaction*. According to VandenBos (2007), abreaction is "the therapeutic process of bringing forgotten or inhibited material (i.e., experiences, memories)

At this point, the volunteer reported feeling a great amount of relief. Although she did not identify what she had experienced, she said that she had indeed gone to the source of her problem, relived the pain involved, and felt a burden had been lifted from her. Afterwards we met and were able to process this event further.

from the unconscious into consciousness, with concurrent emotional release and discharge of tension and anxiety. The term is very closely related to catharsis" (p. 3).

Returning to Consciousness

In order to bring the client out of the hypnotic state I count from 1 to 5. I tell them that when they hear "4" they will be awake and at "5" they will open their eyes.

Posthypnotic Session Techniques to Bring About Greater Awareness and Healing

There are many ways you can help facilitate your healing after the therapy session is over. I teach my clients a variety of techniques, and they use what they find most helpful.

Self-hypnosis: Clients learn self-hypnosis to integrate their personal issues uncovered during age regression and to communicate to their unconscious the positive change they are undergoing.

Breathing training: I teach clients breathing techniques to help them to relax and create a more stress-free environment in which to heal; this reduces symptoms. For example, a client who suffers from a phobia may find breathing very helpful in reducing feelings of panic and dizziness.

Posthypnotic suggestions: Posthypnotic suggestions vary depending on the specific needs of the client. For example, for a patient with anxiety or a phobia, I may give a specific suggestion to use during times when he or she feels anxious. I told one client, "Any time you feel anxious, it may be helpful to ground yourself by touching thumb to forefinger in each hand and mentally repeating, 'I am free, calm, and relaxed.'" Clients are generally asked to practice on their own for 5 minutes 5 times a day and increase this to 15 minutes 3 times a day. Eventually they will practice 5 times a day for 15 minutes each time. These suggestions are very useful in modifying unhealthy behaviors or habits; they help with concentration, work productivity, and are helpful for quitting smoking, losing weight, or decreasing anxiety states.

Awareness of feelings, body, and body changes: Clients also learn greater awareness of bodily sensations and feelings. Oftentimes, clients are disconnected from their feelings, and these feelings get stuffed, repressed, and wind up as negative thoughts about the self. These techniques help the client to be more in touch with the body and create wholeness between body and mind.

Together, these tools help clients maintain a state of being calm and relaxed, circumventing worries between sessions and after therapy is over.

Gestalt technique: Sometimes, along with age regression, there is a need to do something to help a client resolve an interpersonal conflict. For example, I had a client who had a conflict with his sister over the money they would receive from an inheritance. Due to the conflict, the client was emotionally cut off from his sister. This means they were no longer speaking due to irresolvable differences. To help him enter the hypnotic state, I counted from 3 to 1. I then told the client that I was going to count from 1 to 3 and at the count of 3, his sister would be sitting in a chair in a few feet in front of him.

With his sister there in the room, the client was able to tell her how he felt and help her to understand his perspective. His sister then responded with her point of view. The conflict was resolved in this way because the client was able to express his anger towards her. Through this process, he also realized that letting her know how he felt would not necessarily make their relationship worse. After this session, the client was able to communicate effectively with his sister, and their conflict was eventually resolved in actuality.

Working through: When clients come back for another session, I ask them about their experiences since our last therapy session. Initially, clients may bring up new material that seems totally unrelated but which is usually connected to their hypnotherapy experience. This is the phase when they are integrating the changes that new knowledge from hypnotherapy brings. This phase of therapy may last from 3 to 16 sessions. If something comes up for them after therapy has ended, they may come back for a few more sessions.

CHAPTER 7

ANXIETY

If we all did the things we are capable of,
we would astound ourselves.

Thomas A. Edison

*Out beyond ideas of right doing and wrongdoing
there is a field.
I'll meet you there.*

~Rumi

In my experience, one of the mental traps that keep us suffering is to imagine that the choices we make are either right or wrong. In order to heal, we need to show compassion for ourselves in our unrealized state, the state we were in before we were able to understand that there is a source of our suffering and a path to healing. I like to think that this is a place where we can stop judging ourselves for what we have done in the past and what has been done to us. As R. P. Butterfly stated in the opening pages of this book, "These behaviors did not make me a bad person; it was just my silent cry of desperation and my way of coping with my pain that made me behave the way I did." In the case below, I will present the story of a client who was very much needing to let go of the wrongs that had been done to him, as well as all the wrongs that he had done to others as a consequence.

More people come to me with anxiety issues than for

any other reason. This may be because anxiety disorders are becoming increasingly prevalent in both the US and around the world. A recent review published by the *Canadian Journal of Psychiatry* found that nearly 17% of the general population suffers from an anxiety disorder during their lifetime. Untreated, anxiety disorders create a great deal of anguish. They can be so debilitating that one's functioning is severely restricted. Studies have suggested that chronic anxiety disorder can lead to death from cardiovascular problems, such as heart attacks. This may be due to the fact that anxiety places continual stress on a person, although the source of the stress is often unknown.

Anxiety produces both emotional and physical distress. According to VandenBos (2007), it is "a mood state characterized by apprehension and somatic symptoms of tension in which an individual anticipates impending danger, catastrophe, or misfortune" (p. 63). This "vague fear of the unknown (e.g., a general sense of impending doom)" (p. 63) may be accompanied by physical symptoms, such as headache, tightness in the chest, restlessness, and perspiration.

The *Synopsis of Psychiatry* distinguishes between anxiety and fear. Fear comes about as a result of a threat that is known. It is nameable, distinguishable, and located outside of one's body. However, with anxiety, the true source of the fear is unknown because it is often caused by an unconscious object or event. Although the source of anxiety is unknown because it is in the unconscious, it is often displaced onto something in the person's outer world. Displacement occurs when one locates a feeling or anxiety onto something or someone in the external world. For example, one may have a fear of an object, or significant person in one's life, such as a parent. That fear then becomes located in an object in the outer world. An example of this would be a woman who fears snakes because she has been molested by her father. However, there are many other examples.

Ali

Ali, a 31-year-old man, was referred to my office by his mother. Ali was born in Afghanistan and came to the US at the age of 3 with his parents. He told me that the reason for his visit was that he was experiencing a great deal of anxiety. He said he was afraid of driving, or even being driven, over a bridge or overpass. His mother reported that most of the time he refused to leave the house and that he also exhibited extreme anger. His mother said that once–when she was about to drive over a bridge–he pleaded with her not to go over it. She answered that the bridge was the easiest way to get to their destination, and he became angry at her and demanded she stop. When she did not stop, he picked up her purse and threw it at her, injuring her hand.

He did not hold a permanent job, and he tended to blame other people for his own failures. He had been a truck driver for a grocery outlet. He explained to me that he had lost his job because his employer would send him to places that were problematic because of road and traffic conditions; nevertheless, they expected timely deliveries. He thought they always gave him the worst routes and the most demanding customers to deal with.

He also thought his parents held unrealistically high expectations for him. When he was in high school, they would tell all their friends how well he was doing in school and that he was applying to the best colleges. In reality, he was doing poorly in school and lacked motivation to continue in higher education. He even dropped out of high school.

When he dropped out of school, his parents were mercilessly critical of him, and he felt that had made matters much worse. He blamed his parents for his inability to be successful academically, socially, and professionally. He could not stay in a relationship for very long and never got married. He lived by himself and refused to take medication for his anxiety or see a mental health clinician. His mother heard that hypnosis was effective in treating anxiety and asked me to work with Ali.

During the first session, I observed that his worldview was greatly affected by his anxiety; he viewed the world as a hostile place. In other words, his perception of reality was distorted. He was unable to deduce others' motivations, attitudes, and thoughts, especially in relation to himself. He also had an impaired ability to make meaningful links between events. People with anxiety tend to select certain aspects of their environment that confirm their worldview. This "selective thinking" serves to prove to themselves that they are justified in their point of view. Consequently, much of the reality of a situation is overlooked, and anything new about the world cannot be taken in. In Ali's case, he thought his past employers singled him out to send on routes that had bad, traffic-congested roads, but he never confirmed with other drivers whether they had similar problems.

Although some people might have reasons for fearing something, much of the time their anxiety has unconscious roots, and many people who suffer from anxiety are unable to talk about why they are anxious. Ali was unable to talk about why he was unable to drive over bridges. To find that out we needed to do an age regression.

During the age regression, I asked him to go to the root of his anxious feelings. When he was in the hypnotic state and going backwards in time, I looked for signs that he was experiencing something important. I looked for changes in his facial expression and breathing. When I noticed these, I asked him to tell me where he was and what was happening.

He said, "I am in the first grade, and I do not like my classmates or my teacher." He continued, "I can't understand what the teacher or other children in the class are saying." He had a language barrier, having not learned English in the years he'd been in the US. He said, "During recess, I am not playing with the other children, but am always by myself. I am bored. I don't like school. I have no friends here, and I don't want to be here. But my parents insist I come. I have told them that I don't want to and have begged them not to make me. They don't listen and they don't seem to care."

We moved forward during the regression and when I asked him where he was, he replied that he was in the fifth grade. He said,

> I am being bullied by a peer. He is a big, fat kid.
> He is constantly calling me names. He makes fun
> of my name, calling me Alison. He pushes me. He
> grabs my backpack, looks through it, and throws
> my lunch on the floor. I am always afraid of the
> bullies in this school. I have asked my father if I

can stay home from school and his response is to take out his belt and hit me.

Through age regression, we discovered that the root of his anxiety was a series of traumas, one layered on top of the other. He suffered the trauma of being isolated from his peers through his language barrier. His parents were unsympathetic and harshly abused him for being weak and resistant. This affected his self-esteem. He did not know how to feel empowered, and so he tried to undermine his parents in other ways. Refusing to go to school became a form of defiance against his parents, which he was never able to let go of. He did poorly in school and eventually dropped out of school to continue this defiance. He also began to use drugs, which, needless to say, failed to alleviate his self-esteem problems. No amount of acting out and resisting the will of his parents would help him feel better or to release the pain of the underlying traumas that were the source of his acting out. His lack of success socially and at work and his development of an anxiety issue show that this pattern of resistance was becoming increasingly worse. His refusal to be driven over the bridge by his mother was another way to try to wrest power from her, especially as she insisted they go over it. Through this symptom, he seemed to be saying, "I will not move forward in my life or find a way to bridge our differences." However, every attempt to resist doing what others wanted him to do only heaped more dire consequences on himself. He was severely restricted in every aspect of life and became utterly dependent on others, as was evident by his need to have his mother chauffeur him. He was at the point where he could no longer function.

Once we had discovered the roots of his anxiety, we used multiple approaches to healing it. He was able to release a great deal of anger and sadness over how isolated, alone, unsupported, and unloved he had felt as a child. Through integrating these experiences, he eventually came to understand that his parents were also having a difficult time adjusting to life in the US. He was able to understand that they were struggling with their own set of traumas and therefore were unable to attend to his problems adequately. They had fled from Afghanistan during the 1980s, which was a time of turmoil and war. Afghanistan had been invaded by the Soviet Union in 1979, and his countrymen became locked in a struggle that would last a decade. Many Afghans left the country at that time, but most had fled to Pakistan and Iran. Ali's parents were lucky to be able to come to the US, but they were isolated from friends and family and felt shattered due to the fracturing of life in their homeland; they were not coping well with their losses.

At the time his father was hitting him with a belt, his parents were also fighting. When Ali was 17, his parents divorced. He had believed that he was the reason they were experiencing marital problems, and through therapy he realized that he had not been at fault. He also discovered that his mother also experienced anxiety driving over bridges, which he had not realized.

In short, he began to understand others' perspectives and learned not to be so invested in his way of seeing things. I taught him several techniques to further help him with his anxiety.

Self-hypnosis: Ali learned visualization techniques to use whenever he began to feel anxious about driving. In the morning when he awoke, he was to spend 5 minutes practicing a visualization. He visualized that he was safe, that he was driving over a bridge, and that he was an excellent driver.

Breathing techniques: I taught Ali breathing techniques as well. These were intended to help him ground himself and reduce his state of anxiety. Through these breathing techniques, Ali was able to manage his tendency to hyperventilate. They also reduced his sensations of dizziness.

Posthypnotic suggestions: I gave Ali suggestions that helped to desensitize him to the experience of driving over a bridge. He practiced on his own 5 times a day for 5 minutes each time. Eventually he began to do them 15 minutes 3 times a day. The suggestion he practiced was, "With each inhale I feel in control and safe to drive, and with each exhale I feel comfortable and at ease."

Through the practice of these techniques and his hypnotherapy sessions, his anxiety decreased to the point that he was able to find a new job and keep it. He also re-ported actually finding pleasure in his work for the first time in his life. He would continue to come into therapy as need-ed, and saw me at least five times after the hypnotherapy sessions had ended. He became much better able to note the signs in his body and his behavior that signified he was becoming anxious. His anxiety had been like a tsunami that would continually flood and devastate his life. He be-came very adept at being able to detect the signs that the tsunami was coming and keep it from consuming him.

CHAPTER 8

TREATMENT OF TRAUMA

*Resources for the struggling ego lie within
the unmapped territory of the unconscious.*

Carl Jung

Rumi, the great Persian poet, said "What I had thought of before as God, I met today in a human being." I believe that Rumi was talking about the enormous capacity humans have to heal and relieve their suffering. I want to confirm what has been attributed to the work of Gil Boyne (1989), a pioneer in hypnotherapy practice, that, "It is possible to transform the lives of people who have been programmed for failure, frustration, and unhappiness" (p. xi) by helping them become conscious of the sources of their suffering and thereby addressing the specter of their guilt and their fear of the unknown.

According to VandenBos (2007), trauma is "an event in which a person witnesses or experiences a threat to his or her own life or physical safety or that of others and experiences fear, terror, or helplessness" (p. 955). Any event that threatens the psyche and engenders fear, terror, or helplessness may have traumatic repercussions. VandenBos added, "Traumas that are caused by human behavior (e.g., rape, assault, toxic accident) commonly have more psychological impact than those caused by nature (e.g. earthquakes)"

(p. 955). This is particularly the case with what has been termed chronic or ongoing trauma, which occurs in cases of childhood abuse, including emotional, physical, and sexual childhood abuse. The effects of trauma may cause "dissociation, confusion, and a loss of a sense of safety. Traumatic events challenge an individual's view of the world as a just, safe, and predictable place" (VandenBos, 2007, p. 955).

Many veterans of the military, as well as civilians, who have survived the terrors of war, experience some symptoms of trauma. Research shows that veterans are often diagnosed with posttraumatic stress disorder (PTSD). Symptoms of PTSD include a reexperiencing of the traumatic event in the form of painful memories, dreams or nightmares, or flashbacks. Reexperiencing may also take the form of repeating the trauma by becoming involved in situations that are likely to reproduce the painful affect that accompanied the original traumatic experience. Survivors of trauma often alternate between experiencing a sense of numbness, in order to defend against the painful experience, and a heightened sensitivity or acute arousal to reminders of the trauma. For example, a car backfiring could trigger a war veteran to be startled because it sounds so much like gunfire. Through hypervigilance, a symptom of PTSD, one is endlessly searching on an unconscious level for cues in the environment that could signal danger. Cues that are innocent enough to other individuals may signify a traumatic event to a survivor. In such a state, a trauma survivor is apt to misinterpret others' motives, and he or she finds it very difficult to trust other human beings. Other symptoms overlap with depression, such as experiencing difficulty concentrating and demonstrating little interest in activities one used to find pleasure in.

Another important symptom is that a trauma survivor might feel guilty for having survived. The mother of a client of mine showed anger at her daughter (the client) for not being aware of the fact that their entire family had been killed in the Holocaust. In fact, the girl never received any Jewish education, her family never talked about the Holocaust, and later in life, her mother even discovered distant relatives in Israel who had survived the Holocaust. While the mother had never discussed the Holocaust or how it had affected their family, she had nevertheless expected her daughter to consciously bear the burden of this legacy, with all of the accompanying feelings, including anger. It is often the case that people are reluctant to talk about trauma; it just seems too terrible to be talked about. Yet it is important to consciously process traumatic experience.

The mother in this case had displaced her own sense of guilt onto her daughter, when it was the mother who had failed to keep the memory and the trauma alive in the consciousness of the family. Displacement is a psychological defense mechanism whereby a person disowns his or her own feelings and places them onto another person. The mother could not bear the family legacy consciously, and so she accused her daughter of acting as though it had not happened. "The work" is in recognizing what isn't talked about, yet which is simultaneously imposed on the individual.

Traumatic incidents and the behavior resulting from them can be seen in hypnotherapy as unfinished business. When "unfinished business" is not resolved, an individual may engage in a number of unwanted behaviors to avoid reminders of the trauma. These may take the form of compulsive behaviors or self-defeating activities that interfere with daily life. Events from the past prevent the individual from developing full awareness in the present. These events also demand energy and affect the quality of the person's life. A person with unfinished business will often experience depression, numbness, and exhaustion. An individual may have difficulty functioning in most areas of his or her life, including sexual activities.

The difficulty in processing trauma lies in the fact that a survivor is so effective at avoiding all emotions associated with the trauma. One's entire psychological system is geared around avoiding these feelings. The traumatic experience is intolerable to the mind because it is too painful. However, the way to process trauma is to find a way to consciously experience the feelings associated with the original traumatic event.

In hypnoanalysis, individuals are able to enter a safe place where they are able to reexperience the traumatic event and the painful feelings that have been avoided. Only then will the intense discomfort begin to subside. When dealing with experiences of traumatic or near-traumatic events, the patient is encouraged to reexperience as much of the intensity of the experience as he or she can bear. This experience helps to free the client to be able to live in the present, to be more emotionally present, and to enjoy life. The individual is able to spend less time unconsciously running from the past. Because depression is such a common occurrence in survivors of trauma, I am going to illustrate the use of hypnosis in healing trauma with a client who came to me with chronic depression.

Frank

Frank was a 51-year old Caucasian man who came to see me because his wife threatened to leave him if he did not get help. His suffering was causing him a great deal of pain and anguish, which was also affecting his entire family. He was unable to sleep, had no energy, and he no longer wanted to do things he had always enjoyed doing, such as watching baseball games with his friends. He was on probation from his job, as he often failed to show up for work, and the family was threatened with foreclosure on their home. Frank was filled with excessive guilt, which is another symptom of depression. He blamed himself for his failures, the likely loss of his house and job, and the toll all of this was taking on his marriage and his family. He had three children but was unable to enjoy any type of meaningful relationship with them. He also reported that he had no appetite and would sometimes think about suicide to end his painful existence. He did not want to consult with a psychiatrist or take any medication for his depression. He believed that the source of all his current symptoms was the impending loss of his job and his home. After the initial interview, we began the work.

I decided to conduct an age regression to discover the origins of the issue. As noted elsewhere, during regressions, I ask clients to focus on the issue at hand and I tell them to go to a time when the problem began. At a certain point, I noticed by his facial cues that he was experiencing something important, and I asked him what was happening.

"How old are you and what are you experiencing?"

"I am 5," he told me in a frightened whisper. "I am hiding behind a couch. Nobody knows I'm here. Dad is on the floor with a gun pointed at him."

"Go ahead," I said in a soft voice, hoping to sound reassuring. He continued to describe what he saw:

I hear police sirens. The apartment is being ransacked and people are going from room to room looking for something. They find me and take me to a strange building. I'm scared. I don't know what happened to my dad. I don't know if I will see him or my mom again. My mom is living on the street. I haven't seen her for a long time.

When an individual experiences such a memory under age regression, it is as though they were experiencing that incident for the first time; for Frank, he was that 5-year old child hiding behind the couch. It is sometimes a wrenching experience for a therapist doing this work, to take in the child's point of view of such a devastating experience. Every aspect of this memory had been a pivotal traumatic event for Frank: the alarming sound of police sirens, seeing his father threatened with a gun and potentially being killed, and the inexplicable presence of the child protective services (CPS), who took him to strange place, a housing facility, where he resided while he awaited placement. He was eventually placed into foster care. During this session, he sobbed uncontrollably at the memory and did quite well at processing these painful experiences. He also continued to fill in the gaps to render a fuller picture of his traumatic childhood.

His father had been a drug addict and had gone to jail, while his mother had been a heroin addict and homeless; she had overdosed on heroin and died when he was 12. He told me that he had trust issues all his life, and he was ashamed to reveal his past history to anyone, especially to his wife. He had repressed all the feelings that were associated with these experiences. Until he experienced the age regression, he had simply never felt them. Eventually he had become so depressed that he could barely function. He had been hopeless that this state of being would change, and he had been thinking of ending his life.

Through his ability to reexperience the traumatic situation that occurred at age 5 and the subsequent emotional experiences he underwent, Frank was able to experience enough acute grief to move on with his life. All these events had had significant ramifications in his life; his parents' drug addiction and desperation, his mother's homelessness and her death when Frank was just 12. At the age of 51, Frank was finally able to face the feelings of them. He was able to work through a great deal of the emotional pain and eventually he was able to return to work. We accomplished this in about six sessions. After about 6 months, his wife sent a thank you card indicating that he was back to work and feeling much better.

Frank's age regression uncovered an extremely traumatic incident associated with other devastating traumas that he had never been able to process, but it is my experience that any discomforting symptoms or behaviors can be traced back to an original traumatic incident or series of events. All traumatic events can be reexperienced so that clients are able to consciously integrate and consider their effects, which eventually helps to decrease their symptoms. In many of the cases I have treated with hypnotherapy, the symptoms have been eliminated altogether. As mentioned earlier, trauma is usually at the source of our suffering. When someone is traumatized and is unable to process the experience, anxiety or depression usually follows.

CHAPTER 9

DEPRESSION

A joy, a depression, meanness,

Some momentary awareness comes

as an unexpected visitor.

Rumi, from "The Guest House"

Depression often occurs due to traumatic events or loss. The symptoms of depression are almost universally familiar to everyone. People withdraw from their lives and their loved ones. They become numb to their feelings; they may either stop eating or overeat, and hence they experience weight loss or weight gain. They often have difficulty sleeping, or they oversleep. They no longer find meaning in life, no longer enjoy even simple pleasures, and feel dull and listless. Psychologists use the term *anhedonia* for the inability to enjoy life so notable in people who are depressed; it is a key symptom of depression. Anhedonia is "the inability to enjoy experiences or activities that would normally be pleasurable" (VandenBos, 2007, p. 53). People who are depressed often cannot concentrate. Depression, in essence, is a sheer absence of joy, life, and vitality. When depression is severe, people become hopeless and are sometimes suicidal.

I had a client with a case of depression that was truly representative of depression in every respect. Mr. P not only had all the symptoms of depression, but the source of his depression that we discovered during hypnosis is also common.

Mr. P

Mr. P, a retired army lieutenant, came to therapy complaining of feeling bored and unmotivated. He said that he had no friends and that he felt that his life had been "on idle and not going anywhere." He had tried working at different jobs to supplement his income as well as to fill his empty time, but none of those jobs appealed to him, and he would eventually quit.

He lived with his wife, and this was his second marriage. He had one son from his previous marriage, and he explained that his relationship with his son was not good. He said that they were not talking to each other, but he did not go into detail about the source of the conflict. Mr. P was not only very reticent about talking about his feelings, he was also relatively cut off from his feelings, a symptom of his depression. He did say that when his first wife had asked him for a divorce, he was never able to address the issue with her or discover her reasons for wanting the divorce; he only got extremely angry over the divorce process. Although he was angry, he remained in contact with his first wife and her next husband. When asked further about why he never addressed his wife's reasons for divorce, he said that he had not wanted to dig into it.

During the session, he looked sad and his eyes watered. Mr. P had been an only child of his biological parents. His father had been an alcoholic and committed suicide when Mr. P was 11 years old. Since his father's death, his mother raised him, and subsequently he became disconnected with his father's side of family. He remembered that at his father's funeral, his grandmother told him that boys from her side of the family do not cry. However, he mentioned that he had cried over his father's death many times.

When Mr. P retired, his mother passed away. He said he missed her a great deal; she had been the only person to whom he had felt truly connected. It was evident that Mr. P had begun to experience depression at this point. He explained that he had come to therapy because he had lost interest in doing most things, even cleaning his room. He no longer spent time with others or did things he once enjoyed, such as going on walks. I asked him the reason he chose hypnotherapy for treatment.

At that point, for one of the first times in the interview, he smiled. He said that long ago when he was on the army football team, he'd suddenly lost motivation and interest in playing. He met with a hypnotherapist, and within a few sessions, he was able to go back and play on the team. He said that he did wonderfully well and was focused. He also said that his desired state was to be happy.

First session. I asked him if he had seen another therapist for his current issues. He said that he'd seen a therapist once during his divorce. He said that that therapist told him that the source of his problem was his alcoholic father and grandfather. He told me he did not like the counselor's explanation and did not return. I asked Mr. P, as I ask all my clients during their first interview, to think of a safe place and a resource he could take with him on his hypnotherapy journey. He said that his safe place was a bank vault. I thought this was an interesting choice. It implied how unsafe Mr. P must have felt. It told me that his depression was partly there because he felt unsafe in a more freed up space. He needed thick heavy walls to protect him and a secret combination for opening that space, which few people could know. It also suggested his need for isolation–that he felt safer in a vault–alone within steel walls. One of the resources he wanted to take with him for safety was a knight. It was another unusual choice. It suggested medieval times and the need for a strong protector in a suit of armor. He mentioned that it would serve him in his crusade. Perhaps, I thought, he would need a crusade to uncover the truth. It was a strange thought but proved to be fitting.

During the age regression, he went to age 4.

"What are you experiencing?" I asked.

He said, "I'm stuck. Nothing is happening."

I had the sense that he was experiencing something traumatic because I observed tremendous changes in his breathing.

"Where is your knight?" I followed.

"The knight is behind me and he is doing nothing," he responded. This meant the knight was useless.

I asked him to move forward in time.

"Where are you now?" I asked.

"I'm relaxing in my house," he answered. He had moved from age 4 to the current time and he had returned to his house.

"What's happening?"

"Nothing," he said.

I had a sense that whatever it was he experienced he did not want to talk about it. I did not believe nothing had been happening either at age 4 or currently, but we were nearing the end of our session, so I brought him out of hypnosis.

"Tell me about your experience under hypnosis," I said. He appeared to be extremely puzzled about his experience and also a bit agitated.

"You should have waited and not rushed me to experience things that I am not ready to experience."

He appeared to be unhappy about what had transpired and told me that I had not made any motivational suggestions like the other hypnotherapist had. He reminded me that a long time ago he had seen a hypnotist to improve his football performance. That time, he had been given suggestions to improve his game. He was told that when he returned to the football field that he would be able to perform at the highest level of his ability. When he told me he did not feel like anything significant had happened with me to help him with his current problems, I reminded him of something we had previously discussed, "This is your journey, go with it."

I asked him if there was anything that he had liked about this session. He said the relaxation induction and deepening induction felt "great." He said that it had made him feel relaxed. He reported that he felt rested and energized. He also complimented me on not making a diagnosis based on his being the son of an alcoholic father. Then he added, somewhat ominously, that his knight was nothing more than a dead statue.

He said he would call back for another appointment if he felt he needed one. He paid for the session and left. I observed him from the window of my office as he got into his truck. He sat in his truck and waited a few minutes before leaving. He did not see me watching, but I saw that his face still looked puzzled. However, I had no real concern about him. I wrote in my journal that he would call for another appointment no later than the following week. In short, I predicted that he would be back.

My wife runs my office and was surprised that no second appointment was made. I really had no clue except I knew things happen in the unconscious mind in very personal, unique ways. I knew that I was a guide and no more than that. It is often enough to know that. I feel that through my practice I give opportunities for clients to discover what is theirs to discover. I never push them—first because I know how strong resistances are—and second, because I have discovered through experience that they must be ready and willing to participate in treatment and choose the treatment that is right for them if the outcome is to be fruitful. However, I was eager to know what he had experienced during that session and where he would be going next. I was not surprised when he called 4 days later to make another appointment. I was very glad that he had decided to come to the second session and intrigued about where his journey would take him.

Second session. Every time I meet with clients, I ask them about their experiences between sessions. This is part of the working through process, which refers to the process of integrating into one's consciousness and life that which had been uncovered in hypnosis and what has subsequently transpired since the last session. Mr. P mentioned that he went to visit his ex-wife in the hospital after she had minor surgery and that he had seen her husband also. Although he had always been angry in the past when meeting with his ex-wife, he reported that he had not been angry at all when he saw her this time. Also, he mentioned that he had cleaned his room and gone for a walk. He asked me what I thought had happened that had created these changes in him.

I reminded him that one of his goals was to be happier. During hypnosis, I had given him a posthypnotic suggestion that he would be happier than before and that his relations with his family would improve. I also gave him the suggestion that he would walk at least 30 minutes a day to improve his health and wellbeing. I reminded him that I had told him before the hypnotherapy procedure that I would make these suggestions and that we had discussed this after he had emerged from hypnosis as well. However, he had not made the connection between his experiences after therapy and the therapy itself. He responded to my reminders with what follows.

Mr. P: "It is that simple?"

T: "That simple, I guess so. It is your experience, your journey, not mine."

Mr. P: "What are we going to do today?"

T: "What problem would you like to resolve today?"

Mr. P: "I don't know."

T: "What brings you here today?"

Mr. P: "I want to continue to feel better."

T: "Would you like to do another age regression?"

Mr. P: "Let's do it," He said with some enthusiasm and a smile.

When Mr. P was in a hypnotic state and I observed rapid eye movement I asked him about his experience.

T: "How old are you?" I asked.

Mr. P: "5."

T: "What are you experiencing?"

Mr. P: "I am in a park."

T: "Describe the park to me."

Mr. P: "There are lots of trees . . ."

T: "Who is there with you?"

I noticed his breathing got faster.

Mr. P: "My mother."

T: "Anyone else?"

Mr. P: "Yes, but I do not see him. He's a shadow."

T: "Stay with your experience."

There was a pause of several minutes.

Mr. P: "Now, we left the park."

T: "Tell me more. Be as detailed about what you are experiencing as possible."

Mr. P: "I am in the car, sitting in the back seat; Mom is in the front seat. Mom is upset."

T: "Who is driving?"

Mr. P: "I can't see. I don't know."

T: "Do you feel safe?"

Mr. P: "Yes, but I'm worried."

T: "Tell me more."

Mr. P: "We're in a meadow, walking on dry leaves, it's very windy. I am going toward a cliff. The wind is too strong and it wants to take me."

T: "Where is your dog?" [Today he had taken a dog with him as a resource.]

Mr. P: "I don't see him. It's too windy–I am being pushed toward the edge of the cliff and lifted off the ground!" Mr. P continued, sounding terrified, "The wind is forcing me to go forward and up, and it is carrying me off the cliff!"

T: "Stay with your experience and tell me the details."

I noticed he was breathing heavily.

Mr. P: "A hand is reaching out to me to prevent me from falling."

T: "Whose hand it is? Do you see the person?"

Mr. P: "It's my dad. He's holding onto me to keep me from falling off the cliff."

T: "Stay with your experience."

Mr. P. "I'm back on the ground. I'm safe."

While he was still under hypnosis during this session,

I made a suggestion that he would be happier, that he would continue to clean his room, and that his connection with people would be better. Then I brought him back to the present time.

When he was out of hypnosis we talked about what had transpired. The person or the shadow he was seeing was actually his father. His father had been with him the whole time, but he had been unable to see him or experience him on a conscious level. The experience in the first session may have also been about his father. Although he was never able to talk about what he had experienced in that first session, I believe his resistance was so strong that he simply refused to consciously take in the experience. It may have also been an experience during which he had felt overwhelmed and with few resources, as indicated by his knight being of no use to him. Or his knight, in its rigid suit of armor, had represented his defenses, which did not allow him the vulnerability he needed to experience what was his to experience.

He also may have had difficulty trusting me because as his therapist I may have reminded him on an unconscious level of his father. In addition, his feeling of being unprotected had been such a strong leitmotif in his life that it may have been difficult to allow such a transformative "new" experience to "invade" his life. His belief that he had been abandoned by his father was a theme that he had built up around him like the walls of a bank vault.

In this story his father had abandoned him. His mother also played notes on this theme when she would tell him his father had been an alcoholic who had been irresponsible and self-serving. It is important to mention here that children who have a parent die when they are young are apt to blame themselves. It is doubly so when a parent commits suicide. A child feels that the parent does not care enough for them to live. Children also feel as though the bad things that happen around them are their fault. They must hold themselves responsible because it is too threatening to live in a world where such catastrophic things can happen at any time for no reason. Thus, even during the second hypnosis session, as Mr. P went back in time to an early experience, he was unable to really "see" his father and know he was there. This was a metaphor for how, after his father's death, he had been unable to grasp his father as a loving, beneficent force.

When, during hypnosis, he was falling over the cliff, he clearly saw that it was his father holding his hand and keeping him from falling. When I had asked him to,"stay with your experience" he reported, "I am on the ground. I am safe." It may have been one of the first times in his life he experienced that kind of safety. It was to become a new metaphor for his father's role in his life, especially needed at this juncture, when he really needed to feel his protective presence.

Through hypnosis he was able to experience this presence. He realized his father had been with him throughout his life and that his father's suicide was not his fault. His father had committed suicide when he was 11, so his being able to access the early experience of his father saving him was transformative. During hypnosis I saw his affect: His face reflected such enormous relief. A life's burden had truly been lifted from him.

Mr. P had said, "Wow. I always . . . I always knew that.

We used to go to the woods and the cliff. But I never realized that my father really saved me. It was always so windy and I would stand on the cliff. But this time I saw my father hold my hand so I did not fall." In other words, he had always had the memory, but he did not have the affect or meaning of it, and the whole of it had been buried underneath the strong leitmotif of his life that his father had abandoned him. Mr. P was thus able to go back and experience the meaning of the real presence of his father in his life, and this helped to transform all of the distorted thinking that had occurred in the wake of his father's suicide.

After this session, we continued to work through his feeling of having been abandoned by his father. He was also able to talk about his mother. She had died at the age of 84, and he had experienced her as very caring. But he also began to realize that they had had difficulties in their marriage, and she had passed on some of her resentment about his father onto him. He also came to understand that she had kept him from connecting with his father's side of the family, and this had served to help bury the memory of his father and to keep the "aliveness" of his presence out of his life. He subsequently began to reconnect with his father's side of the family. He also began to socialize, meet new people, and by the time he left therapy, he had made many new friends.

CHAPTER 10

ADDICTION

*The only time I can be in harmony with
anything is when I am in harmony
with myself.*

Hazrat Pir Nader Shah Angha,

Sufi Master

141

Addiction can come in many forms; it can manifest as cravings for food, alcohol, stimulation, or work. Most people try to suppress these urges through sheer willpower. However, willpower will not work because the unconscious has been flooded with negative thoughts and feelings due to past trauma. These eat away at one's will to change. If you do not face the incidents of the past that have created the poisonous atmosphere in your unconscious, you will not be able to be happy, be free, or accomplish the goals you set for yourself. Traumatic experience sets up stressful conditions in the unconscious mind, which are much more powerful than willpower. Stress has been known to deplete willpower and make it impossible for some people to achieve their goals.

Therefore, people can fail to meet every goal they set for themselves, and the negative cycle continues as they berate themselves for failing. I'm going to give you a sense of the first three sessions in my office with Victor to exemplify how hypnotherapy helped a man who was alcoholic and so depressed at his sense of failure, worthlessness, and being a "loser," that he was suicidal.

Victor

Victor came to me because he was about to lose everything. His marriage was failing, and his job was at risk. He was addicted to alcohol, and he would get so inebriated at night that he would have to call in to work "sick" in the morning. His daughters were getting into trouble at school, and he felt responsible for their behavior. He admitted to me that at times he had thoughts that he no longer wanted to continue living.

The first thing I did was make sure that he was safe and unlikely to act on these thoughts. I wanted to make sure that he had plenty of resources in case these thoughts came up between sessions. Although he earned a very good living in the construction industry as a laborer, he was convinced he was a loser. His unconscious had undoubtedly gotten the message because he was about to lose his job, his marriage, and his family. He said that he drank in order to relax and to be able to sleep at night. He said that when he drank he would feel physically numb, but the alcohol was unable to numb his negative thoughts, which persisted. He told me his desired physical state was to be calm, relaxed, focused, and healthy. Mentally, he wanted to be more engaged with his family, participate in his children's school activities, and spend more quality time with his wife. I told him,

> You need to love and like yourself first . . . Take care of yourself, and automatically you will care for your family. What I got from what you have told me is that you are a caring father and a family man. That's why you are committed to working on and resolving your issues. You are trying to face the reason you are in such a difficult situation right now. Being aware of what is happening with your life is the first step.

I asked Victor whether he had had any prior experience with therapy or hypnosis. He said, "A friend came to see you to stop smoking and he was successful at quitting through hypnotherapy. I was really impressed by his success and thought hypnotherapy might work for me to quit drinking." He said he had been in various treatment programs. He had been in inpatient treatment as well as a 12-step program for his alcohol addiction, but he claimed that these had failed to work for him. He also denied that he had an alcohol addiction. He had tried quitting before for 2-3 weeks at a time but decided to drink again. I should mention here that this happens quite often. An alcoholic convinces himself that he doesn't have a problem because he is able to abstain for a period of time. Victor, likewise, had convinced himself that he was capable of quitting at any time. In spite of denying he was an alcoholic, he was asking for my assistance to quit drinking, and I saw that as a sign he was willing to change.

I explained to him how hypnosis worked and told him that through hypnosis he would access his unconscious mind and would discover the reason he had difficulty giving up alcohol. I asked him if he was ready to be hypnotized, and when he responded positively, I helped him to enter a state of hypnosis. I asked him to go to his safe place. I then helped him enter a deeper hypnotic state required for the age regression. When I noticed something happening, I asked him how old he was, and he told me he was 5. He told me his mom was cooking, his younger sister was in the room, and he was playing. I asked if he felt safe.

"Yes," he said.

"Where is your dad?" I asked.

"At work," he said. I asked him to progress forward in time. When I saw from his body tension and eye movements that he was experiencing something, I asked him again to tell me his age.

"I'm 10. I'm in a classroom at school. I like this teacher. In fact I like all my teachers. I have friends and we have a great time playing at recess."

When I asked him whether he felt safe, he said, "Yes." We then progressed again upwards in age. I now asked him to go to the age when he started to feel unsafe. He told me he was in middle school at age 13.

"I don't like this school," he told me. "I don't have many friends, and the other kids are bullying me. I ask a girl that I like to the dance, and she tells me no. I like the girls, but they don't want to talk to me. I feel alone all the time."

In pubescence, he was overweight and evidently unattractive to his peers. His mom was continually cooking and encouraging him to eat, and he was eating because something had been going wrong.

"What are you doing now?" I asked.

"I'm going home," he answered.

"Is anyone with you?" I asked.

"No," he said.

"What are you feeling?" I asked.

"I feel angry."

He described the situation at home. "My mom is cooking and Dad is not home. I'm at the refrigerator picking up a can of my dad's beer. It tastes good. It makes me feel good."

From this memory, we discovered that the root of addiction began in middle school. Evidently from an early age he associated his mom's cooking with safety, which may have been the reason he overindulged in food. His being overweight caused others to tease him and was a source of negative feelings towards himself. His dad's role in his trauma had yet to unfold.

In the second session we discovered that another critical piece of the trauma was his dad, who was not home in each memory he had visited in the first session. His father was in the military and had unrealistically high expectations for Victor academically and athletically. Victor had failed to meet these expectations. Although he was capable of excelling in school, being overweight prevented him from performing well in sports. His failure to please his dad lowered his self-esteem still further, and this affected his performance in school. His dad was harsh and he felt unloved by him. Victor responded by going to his mom for affection, who tried to comfort him with her home cooked meals. He had been trying to numb his feelings of hurt and anger through food and alcohol ever since. He adopted his dad's attitudes towards himself and inwardly held unrealistic expectations for himself. These expectations accounted for his stubborn insistence that he was a loser.

Once these memories were uncovered, Victor was able to begin to work through his true feelings toward his father.

It was the beginning of transforming his life so that he no longer needed alcohol to cope with his feelings of anger and low self-esteem. As his feelings of self-regard increased, so did his ability to find true satisfaction with his family.

CHAPTER 11

WEIGHT MANAGEMENT

Don't get lost in your pain,
know that one day
your pain will become
your cure.

Rumi

Many times, people who come to me to lose weight discover that underlying issues have created obstacles in their ability to achieve their desired weight. In their minds, they know overeating is harmful to their health, and they often feel that being overweight is a reflection on themselves. They may worry that others will judge them for being overweight. People often think that when someone is overweight they have no self-control or do not care enough about their health to eat right.

The key to unleashing your inner healer for losing weight is to discover what is in the unconscious mind that wants you to stay overweight. Oftentimes, security is an issue. As Elman suggested in *Hypnotherapy*, the search for security takes one

> back to the time when oral satisfaction repre-
> sented complete security–when mother fed and
> took care of them. They eat, and continue to eat,
> because eating gives them the sense of security
> which allays a fear lurking below the level of
> conscious awareness. (p. 167)

Being thinner can also make one feel more vulnerable. This chapter is for people who eat due to emotional factors.

Every patient has his or her different reason for being fearful, and the hypnotherapist works with each individual to locate the source of the fear. I can give you an example based on a client that came to me because she was overweight. Her testimonial is in the "Letter From a Client" at the beginning of this book, and here I will explain more about how and why hypnotherapy helped her. I will call her R. P. Butterfly.

R. P. Butterfly

R. P. Butterfly came to me complaining of a strained relationship with her husband. She said that her problems with her husband stemmed from the fact that her husband wanted to have sex with her, but she wanted to avoid it. She said she wished she wanted to have sex with him because she loved him deeply, but there was also something preventing her from wanting it. She had not even been able to have sex with him on their honeymoon. She said she had been ashamed at how her naked body appeared. She was also concerned about how she was treating her two children, ages 10 and 12. She would constantly get angry at them and worried about the effect this was having on them. She also said she could not bring herself to clean her home or to actively look for work. She had been a successful investor in real estate. She had made several purchases in real estate; however, she lost them due to the collapse of the housing market. She was also concerned because she was gaining weight in spite of the fact that she had had gastric bypass surgery several years earlier. These were all symptoms of depression.

I asked what her desired state was and she said it was to be slim. I explained to her how hypnosis worked and the procedure of age regression. I used Freud's iceberg model of the mind (see page 13) to explain the structure of her mind to her and the importance of finding out what was in her unconscious that was impeding her from losing weight and from wanting to have sex with her husband.

I taught her to relax her mind by using progressive relaxation, and then I used an elevator induction to bring her into a deeper hypnotic state. With this induction, when the client goes down in the elevator she or he is going further back in time.

I told her, "You are in an elevator on floor 10, and we will go down the elevator. You may choose to stop at any floor you wish." The floors were counted: 10, 9, 8, and so on, and R.P. Butterfly stopped at the lobby. She got out. She walked a bit onto the floor and said it was too crowded. She got back into the elevator and pushed the button of the third floor. When she got off the elevator, she proceeded to one of the hotel rooms and saw her husband sleeping there. She walked out, went back to the elevator, and this time she went to Parking Level 2. She got out with a little trepidation.

"I'm lonely and I'm scared," she said. She had taken Jesus with her for her support. Because of this support, she said she felt safe in spite of feeling scared. She saw a girl who was 5 years old.

The girl was chubby and she had buck teeth. She thought this girl was beautiful, but this girl was running away from her. She followed her, and they entered a huge garden.

"Come toward me," she said, and then she held the little girl in her arms. Then she started to cry.

"Stay with your experience," I said. "What do you want to tell her?"

I knew by what was transpiring that the girl symbolized an aspect of herself she needed to heal. She was an injured part of R. P. Butterfly.

"How do you want to heal her?" I added.

She told the girl that she was safe, while holding her to her chest. She nourished her with love, all the while crying. She had been lying on the couch with her face turned away from me. Now, she turned her face towards me. She explained later that she had felt safe. Healing the little girl had helped her to feel safe for the first time around a man. I brought her out of the hypnosis induction and she talked about her experience.

She said she had been abused by her uncle many, many times, and when she had brought it up to her mother and father, they had not believed her. This explained why when she was on her honeymoon she could not bring herself to have sex with her husband. Reliving the trauma that she experienced early on through hypnotherapy had been extremely healing for her. She told me that she had always known what had happened but that she had not been able to truly face it nor find compassion for the part of her that had been wounded.

Sometimes I find the healing transformation that my clients undergo is so profound that words simply cannot adequately capture what transpires. However I will try to use simple language to explain something of what I believe happened in the healing of R. P. Butterfly.

When someone has been sexually abused, it is one of the most crippling traumatic events a person can endure. It affects individuals on multiple levels. This wounding is particularly severe to one's sense of self, one's sense of worthiness as a human being, and one's self-esteem. R. P. Butterfly had blamed herself for what had happened to her. When an adult molests a child, it is inconceivable to the child. Children cannot believe that they can be so unprotected by the people who are supposed to care for them that such a thing could happen. When her parents failed to believe her account of what had happened to her, she felt deeply betrayed and even more unprotected. The trauma was humiliating, and in some ways, the betrayal by her parents was worse. A child depends so much on her parents for survival that it is impossible to consciously blame them for such terrible events. The child therefore blames herself.

R. P. Butterfly heaped blame on herself unconsciously and continued to blame herself for all the things that happened as a result of the abuse. When she could not have sex with her husband, she blamed herself. When she failed to maintain a healthy weight in spite of the gastric bypass, she blamed herself. She was filled with self-loathing for the humiliation she endured, which mired her in self-destructive, self-defeating thoughts and desires.

She ate in order to numb the feelings of shame and humiliation that the abuse had left her with. Under hypnosis, she was able to face her innocence for the first time. The child with buck teeth had them through no fault of her own.

The child was scared and ran away from her, from R. P. Butterfly and her own past. R. P. Butterfly was able to tearfully hold herself for the first time and feel on a deep level what had happened. Moreover, she was able to recognize her own beauty. As she wept all of the tears for herself that had never been wept, she was at last forgiven by the very person from whom she needed it the most, herself.

For the rest of the therapy she continued to feel better and the healing she had experienced during hypnotherapy gave her much more compassion for her wounded self. This healing extended to her relationships with her husband and children. She was able to enjoy sex with her husband for the first time. She started a business helping people to solve their financial issues; after losing her houses and suffering through the financial crisis, she was equipped to help other people rebuild their lives. Her letter to me, which discusses her profound experience in hypnotherapy, is a testament as much to her strength and spiritual resilience as it is to the healing power of the techniques in this book.

CHAPTER 12

SELF-HYPNOSIS

You will Wake,

And Remember

And Understand.

Robert Browning

Once your inner healer has been activated by the practitioner in therapy, the techniques of self-hypnosis allow your healer to further the process. Self-hypnosis can be defined as a light state of hypnosis in which the client enters a deep state of relaxation and the mind becomes ego-receptive. In this state, the unconscious mind is susceptible to the positive suggestions that you give it.

Clients use self-hypnosis in order to make suggestions to their minds to accelerate their healing. Self-hypnosis, therefore, includes many different techniques, including posthypnotic suggestions that have been touched upon in previous chapters. The techniques are designed to fit the unique needs of the client. In other words, whatever is most appropriate and effective in helping the client achieve a deep state of relaxation is used to overcome his or her particular issues.

I teach clients self-hypnosis in the first session. At that point they may begin to use self-hypnosis at home and continue as often as they want. However, clients usually begin to effectively utilize self-hypnosis after the third session. Self-hypnosis is particularly useful after the therapy has ended. Clients continue to use self-hypnosis and progress with their healing for as long as they need to. In short, self-hypnosis becomes incorporated in their daily routines. These techniques are safe to use, have no side effects, and they leave you feeling very good and very relaxed.

As self-hypnosis is utilized primarily in the last phases of hypnotherapy, it is important to remember that these procedures and autosuggestions will not be successful unless all other important phases of the work have been carried out. First, the groundwork must be prepared by the creation of a safe, honest, nurturing relationship between the client and therapist so that the client is able to uncover the source of his or her symptoms and begin to prepare for the planting of new seeds of healing. Any resistance to change must also be addressed. Also, these techniques should not be used until clients have uncovered and processed the underlying issues that have brought them to therapy. In other words, autosuggestions can only "work" after clients have processed their trauma during the hypnotic state and in the working through process with the support of the therapist. Once these phases have been accomplished, the appropriate seeds, or suggestions, which have been collaboratively prepared by the client and therapist, can be planted. They will hopefully take root in the unconscious mind, where they will have transformative effects.

I train my clients to do self-hypnosis in four phases (words in italics are in Farsi, my native Persian language).

1. *Hadaf* (Set your desire goal)

2. Relax your body and mind

3. *Talghin* (Suggestions)

4. Visualization

First phase

In this phase, the client's goal must be clear and transparent; it must be verbally and cognitively explained, doable, and achievable. I advise you to write it down and commit it to memory. Make sure that this goal is something that can be measured in concrete ways. Having a specific system of measurement will leave little room to question whether or not your goal has been achieved.

Second Phase

The second phase helps you to achieve a state of relaxation that is so critical to the hypnosis process. The state of relaxation must extend to both body and mind. The more relaxed your body and mind are, the more your unconscious will be susceptible to the suggestion you will give it. In this phase you will be relaxed and alert. It is in this state that the "chatterbox" conscious mind slips into the background, and the unconscious mind comes to the foreground and is highly open to receiving suggestions. Thus, real change or shifts can happen.

I teach the following technique for relaxation of mind and body for the purposes of self-hypnosis:

Take a long, deep, breath.

Inhale and exhale as follows: The ratio between inhalation and exhalation should be 1: 1-1/2 (e.g., count to four as you inhale and to six or seven as you exhale and get all the air out).

Do this at least five times.

(When you are breathing deeply in this way, you will be inhaling and exhaling approximately four-five times each minute).

Close your eyes and relax.

While you are slowly inhaling and exhaling, pay attention to the muscles in and around your eyes.

If your eyes are slightly open, relax them to the point that they are unfocused.

Allow your eyelids to become heavier and more relaxed.

At this point, begin to count backward from 100.

This will give your mind a simple task to do so that other thoughts can begin to diminish. In other words, this exercise helps you to relax mentally.

As you silently say each number, pause momentarily until you feel a wave of relaxation cover your body from the top of your head to the tips of your toes.

When you feel this wave of relaxation, then say the next number.

Each time you say a number, you will double the relaxation you had before you said the number.

If these steps are carried out correctly, the numbers that you are counting will begin to fade away. Allow them to simply drop out of mind, and proceed with the next phase.

Third Phase

This is the stage where you begin to make autosuggestions to your unconscious mind. The words and sentences that you use as suggestions should be specific, logical, acceptable, and positive. These suggestions will have been formulated from looking critically at your problem state and your desired state. You insert the set of suggestions into your mind at least 10 times. For example, if I had insomnia and I were looking for deeper, rejuvenating sleep I would say, "With each inhale and exhale I sleep comfortably, easily, effortlessly and healthily. I wake up on time, alert, feeling happier, focused, and refreshed."

Fourth Phase

In the fourth phase I recommend using a visualization of how it will feel once your goal has been reached. In this stage, you use your entire mind, body, and spirit to visualize the way you want to be. Remember, it is important to have conviction that the suggestions are effective, that they are working for you, that you are continually progressing, and that your goals are achievable. The visualization accompanies the specific suggestion(s) you have planted. You simply visualize how you want to see yourself when you have successfully achieved your desired state.

When you first practice the visualization, you may start by verbalizing every aspect of your visualization. For example, Ali, my client whose anxiety prevented him from being able to drive over a bridge, began with closing his eyes and saying these words while he imagined this beautiful imagery: "I am calm, I am relaxed, and I enjoy driving. The sky is blue, the sun is shining, I see billowy white clouds and boats in the water. I am extremely happy to be alive and enjoying this great moment. I use every opportunity to realize all of my potential."

You may begin this process by saying these words to yourself while you visualize, and then eventually you will be able to visualize this imagery without verbalizing. When you use this technique on your own, you will be able to automatically return to the visualization and use all of your senses to experience it at any time you choose. Clients begin their practice of self-hypnosis in my office where I am able to watch their body cues and determine whether or not they have achieved a state of light hypnosis. I give them feedback and make corrections as they master the technique.

I will show how self-hypnosis was used by a client named Daniel who came to see me because of anxiety.

Daniel

Daniel came in because he wanted to take the medical school exam and the idea of taking it filled him with dread. Daniel was a very attractive Persian American man in his

20s. I asked Daniel to describe his problem state and his desired state. He said he felt anxious and overwhelmed at the thought of taking the exam. On a physical level, when he imagined taking the test, he experienced stiffness in his body, especially in his neck; he felt hot, perspired profusely, and his mouth became dry. At the same time he became light-headed and his mind went blank, which he likened to a blank computer screen. His desired state was to be calm and to know that he had learned all the material sufficiently to pass the exam. He also wanted to realize that he did not have to be perfect. He said in his desired state he would feel peaceful, as he does when working in his garden; he would feel good, in control, and be able to let go of his anxiety. He wanted to understand that tests simply let him know how he is doing.

After his first session, I asked him to journal about his experience. I think his experience can give the reader a good sense of how someone experiences hypnosis for the first time. He wrote the following:

Today I underwent a session of hypnotherapy for the first time. I went in without any expectations—

I really did not know what to expect. I have seen popular hypnotism done on television for entertainment, and have even seen some amazing things done, but that was it. I did not know what was possible under it. My hypnotherapist asked what outcome I would like to see from these sessions, to which initially I did not have a definite answer. I stated that I would like to know more about how my mind works, and what it is capable of accomplishing. Looking back, I guess I was asking for an instruction manual for my brain/ mind, something that has constantly eluded me.

Growing up, my biggest obstacle was fear. This was not always the case, however. The first real bout of anxiety that I remember began on my first days of school in the fourth grade, when I was 8-years old, and it progressed every year until it I began to feel nausea in middle school and would vomit during the first weeks of high school. By the end of high school, I was drained, both emotionally and physically, and I did not want to start university right away. I was 17 when I started UC Santa Cruz, and my parents had high expectations of me; they have always had high expectations of me.

During our session, I was taken back to the second grade. I remembered being inside the classroom watching a movie on the importance of exercise. I remember it was a cartoon and the kids were playing ball, jumping rope, etc. I do not remember much, but I remember I did not associate myself with those children. Then there was a scene of a penguin that was constantly tired and wanting to sleep; he had a nightcap on and went to bed. I felt as though because I did not associate myself with those kids playing outside, I may end up like that penguin—always tired. But I did not know what to do about it. I was not good at sports so I did not enjoy playing outside. I believe my ability to make friends with my schoolmates suffered greatly as a result.

I then thought about a time when I was in the third grade. I enjoyed the third grade very much. I was mature-minded for my age, I behaved well, and some of the girls liked that. I remember one constantly wanted to hang out with me, and people said I had a girlfriend. Since I was a child and did not care about such things, I got mad at the idea and did not want to hang out with her anymore.

Thinking about those times in the past made me feel angry. Now that I am thinking about it some more, I believe my anxiety is due to the high expectations my parents have always had of me. Actually, everyone in my family, both immediate and extended, treated me like a little adult. They rarely treated me like a child.

Perhaps their high expectations led to me having high expectations of myself, to the point where I cannot tolerate failure, or worse, I developed a fear of failure, which led to feeling anxious during potentially stressful situations. I developed both a social anxiety and an anxiety towards coping with life's challenges in general, such as reaching my professional goals. I would like to see my fear and hesitance turned into confidence and empowerment.

Through hypnotherapy, Daniel realized he was anxious over succeeding and failing. He was afraid to succeed because that would mean he would be under his parents' thumbs. It might mean he was doing everything just for them. He really wanted to do what was best for himself. He wondered whether succeeding on this exam would be for them or for himself. He was also very afraid of failing. He wondered deep down whether he was really good enough to be a doctor. However, the important thing was that he had identified the crux of his anxiety, and while we would continue to work through his dilemma, he could better deal with his anxiousness over the exam.

Autosuggestion: Together we came up with a suggestion that he could insert into his mind after going through the procedures described above, which would help him enter a state in which his unconscious mind would be receptive to the suggestion. Daniel used the following suggestion (the italicized words place emphasis on the key words he used to describe his desired state. The suggestion also creates a state opposite to his problem state):

"I enjoy taking exams because they allow me to understand how much *knowledge I have.* As soon as I enter the exam room and sit in my chair, I am *focused, calm,* and *relaxed.* During the exam I remain *alert, clearheaded,* and *able to think.* The muscles of my *neck* are *relaxed* and my *mouth* is comfortable and *moist."*

Visualization: Daniel also used a visualization in the self-hypnotic state. He visualized a computer that stored all that he had learned. He reminded himself that every time he read something or took in some new information it would all be etched into the memory of the computer. He then suggested to himself, "This information is easily accessible whenever I want or need it. During exams I am able to visualize the computer and go in and access the information I need."

Along with visualizing the computer, which would help him access any information he needed, he was reminded that he could go to his safe place if he felt the least bit anxious. From our work together, he had created a safe place that he frequently used to relax. From that place, he would be able to ask any question he wished from his wise, intelligent part of himself. If he had a challenging question, he could simply put the question to this part of himself and move on with the exam, allowing his wise, intelligent mind to formulate the best response while he answered other questions. Eventually the answer would emerge.

Breath training: Daniel also had a technique he used before and during exams. As soon as he entered the exam room, he would take five relaxing, deep breaths. Upon exhaling, all the muscles of his neck and body would relax, pleasantly, and all the tension in his body would leave. At his first view of the test, he was to take three long, satisfying breathes, concentrating only on relaxing the body. As he became deeply relaxed, he would enter a state where his mind was even more fully alert and aware, running at full efficiency.

These exercises gave Daniel the confidence he needed that he was able to rise to the challenge of taking the exam. He was aware that he had tools and resources and could consciously choose his path forward in life.

CHAPTER 13

CONCLUSION

The healing of any wounds,
physically and metaphysically,
is based on acquiring a state of
balance and equilibrium between
the physical state of consciousness
and existential healing powers.

Hazrat pir Nader Shah Angha

I have written this book to acquaint the reader with the process of hypnosis and how it can play a role in transforming individuals' lives. I have been privileged to help many people make this journey from places of severe pain to finding unsurpassed health and success. I find it difficult to put into words just how profound this experience has been for me. Although it is hard to explain why hypnotherapy is so transformative, my clients' stories are testament to its power to heal. I have given the best explanation I could find from among the many psychologists and psychiatrists who have practiced this profession and who have articulated well how it works and why it works.

We all have a great, untapped potential in our unconscious minds. Simply put, if we do not discover what is under the surface of our conscious minds and thoughts, we often leave it to our unconscious to dictate to us the quality of our lives. It takes courage to face what we have been unable to face, to unearth what we have buried deep in the dark recesses of our minds. And I heartily recommend that if you engage in such an undertaking find support from a practitioner who knows the way there and can help you make sense of what you find. Ultimately what is found there is pure treasure. Once accepted into your life, these parts of yourself, long buried beneath the pain of repressed memories, can bring you to a greater state of wholeness. I believe each person has his or her own unique life's journey. The extent to which you risk exploring your buried past is the extent to which you will experience emotional relief and spiritual unfolding. Self-actualization and self-realization are possible if we have the right tools, the right support, and the right attitude of mind.

Last year, I buried dead tulip bulbs
in the ground;
this year they came to life,
so beautiful.
Who is the gardener?

Parviz Shafaghi

Author's Biography

I was born in Persia, also known as Iran, an ancient country that has undergone multiple changes in the last century. Even the name of the country I was born in is a controversial subject for many of us. Much is not known in the West about my birth country. Although the revolution and the oppression are well-known, little is known about the positive, transformational changes that our social life there has undergone in my lifetime. These involve the rapidly evolving social structure; the role of government, which has increasingly played a more active, supportive role in people's lives; the increasing emphasis on education; the broadening of education to include women; and the influence of Western culture on our culture.

I was able to embrace these changes and use them to better myself in order to support others. I finished high school and got a degree in the natural sciences, biology, and through an exit exam, was able to obtain a student visa through the American embassy in the capital. I was accepted by one of the universities near Washington, D.C. and later transferred to American University in Washington, D.C. There I studied biology and took premed classes. Later, I transferred to Stony Brook University in New York State, where I studied psychology and graduated with a BA in psychology.

After many years of practicing on the East Coast, I came to California, pursued my graduate studies at Sacramento State University, and earned a Master's degree in counseling in order to work with individuals, couples, families, and children. Eventually, I earned my doctorate degree in clinical psychology from American School of Professional Psychology, San Francisco Bay Area. It was at Stony Brook University in 1979, the year of the revolution in Iran, that I was introduced to hypnotherapy. However, my interest in hypnosis had begun years earlier in Iran.

When I was in Sufism school, my master took me to visit another student of his who was gravely ill; he was dying of colon cancer. The student's affect was sad; he was hopeless. His face reflected how much pain he was in. My master talked to him in a low tone but with a strong, confident voice for a few minutes and gradually the gravely ill man went into a hypnotic state. During that state, I could see him becoming so relaxed it was as though he had taken some kind of tranquilizing drug. His affect became bright and full of life. I can remember noticing that he was clearly not experiencing any pain. I learned that his cancer was advanced; however, my master was able to teach him techniques to help him accept the fact that disease is part of human life and can be managed.

I had been very impressed with what I had seen in the healing of that student, who lived for a long time regardless of his deadly illness. When I asked my Sufi spiritual master about his healing powers, he said that it was the power of the divine source that healed the patient. He would not credit his work to himself or to any discipline; he was very humble. He mentioned that with patience and attentiveness that I, too, would do creative work. Coming to America helped to fulfill this promise, as I found my passion for psychology and the science of hypnotherapy developing and evolving. Under my master's tutelage, I learned how to be patient, to observe, and to understand the healing power at work in everyone. I am deeply grateful to have been able to help many people to overcome their issues since then. This initial experience with my master, along with my subsequent experiences practicing hypnotherapy with my clients, led me to the place where I can truly say, "Yes I believe in miracles." I have seen many.

GLOSSARY OF TERMS

Abreaction: "The therapeutic process of bringing forgotten or inhibited material (i.e., experiences, memories) from the unconscious into consciousness, with concurrent emotional release and discharge of tension and anxiety. The term is very closely related to catharsis" (VandenBos, 2007, p. 3).

Anhedonia: "The inability to enjoy experiences or activities that would normally be pleasurable" (VandenBos, 2007, p. 53). This is a symptom of depression.

Anxiety: Anxiety is a state involving both physical symptoms of tension and emotional symptoms. A person may sense something terrible is about to happen. The body reacts as if trying to brace itself against the threat, with rapid breathing, rapid heart beat, and perspiration.

Autosuggestion: Autosuggestion is used when using self-hypnosis. Once one carries out the procedures wherein one enters a state of light hypnosis, autosuggestion is used to carry specific messages to the unconscious mind. Through autosuggestion, you are planting thoughts associated with your desired state into your unconscious.

Catharsis: Similar to abreaction, catharsis is the release of emotion, which is "connected to traumatic events that had previously been repressed by bringing these events back into consciousness and reexperiencing them" (VandenBos, 2007, p. 153).

Conscious mind: The ego. The part of the mind that makes decisions. VandenBos (2007) wrote, "In the classical psychoanalytic theory of Sigmund Freud, the region of the psyche that contains thoughts, feelings, perceptions, and other aspects of mental life currently present in awareness" (p. 218).

Depression: Depression is a state of feeling low and dispirited, which is experienced by many people. One of the most common symptoms is anhedonia, which means that one no longer finds pleasure in activities one used to enjoy. A person who is depressed has no enthusiasm for life and tends to withdraw from socializing. VandenBos (2007) wrote that depression is "dysphoria that can vary in severity from a fluctuation in normal mood to an extreme feeling of sadness, pessimism, and despondency" (p. 269).

Desired state: This is the state you want to achieve through hypnotherapy. Clients describe this state by verbalizing how they will feel emotionally when this state is achieved, how they will feel physically, and what thoughts will be in their mind when in this state.

Ego receptivity: Describes the state of mind of one under hypnosis. "In ego receptivity, critical judgment, strict adherence to reality orientation, and active, goal-directed thinking are held to a minimum, and the person allows himself to let unconscious and preconscious material float freely into his mind" (Brown & Fromm, 1986, p. 202).

Free association: A technique used in psychoanalysis and hypnoanalysis in which a patient is told to say whatever comes to mind. It is a way to help the patient and analyst access the unconscious mind.

Hypnosis: A state where the mind is quiet and calm, yet alert. The procedure by which this state of mind is brought about.

Induction: The procedure by which a state of hypnosis is brought about.

Preconscious mind: In Sigmund Freud's theory, "the level of the psyche that contains thoughts, feelings and impulses not presently in awareness, but which can be more or less readily called into consciousness" (VandenBos, 2007, p. 720). Examples include a recent memory.

Primary process thinking: Thinking associated with the unconscious mind. Events can occur at the same time, with no recognition of past and future, and no time; illogic occurs, and images predominate. Contradictions often occur and images and words can have multiple meanings.

Problem state: This is the state you wish to heal or change. Clients describe this state by verbalizing how they feel emotionally when in this state, how they feel physically, and what thoughts are in their mind when in this state.

Secondary process thinking: Secondary process thinking is associated with the conscious mind, as opposed to primary process thinking, which characterizes the thinking of the unconscious mind. In secondary process thinking, logic predominates, and past, present, and future are separate. Events occur in a linear fashion and are determined by cause and effect. The past and the future cannot occupy the same space.

Self-hypnosis: A light state of hypnosis where the client enters a deep state of relaxation and the mind is ego-receptive. In this state, the unconscious mind is susceptible to the positive suggestions that are given it. This state is induced through various techniques taught by the therapist, which are performed by the client during and after therapy.

Unconscious mind. In Freud's theory, the part of the psyche that is not "directly accessible to awareness" (VandenBos, 2007, p. 966) but which has a great influence on feelings, thoughts, and behavior. This region of the psyche contains repressed memories, wishes, and impulses, many of which may appear threatening to the conscious mind for a variety of reasons.

REFERENCES

Boyne, G. (1989). *Transforming therapy: A new approach to hypnotherapy.* Glendale, CA: Westwood Publishing.

Breur, J., & Freud, S. (2009). *Studies on hysteria* (J. Strachey Ed. & Trans.). New York, NY: Basic Books. (Original work published 1981). Retrieved from http://archive. org/stream/studiesonhysteri037649mbp/studiesonhysteri037649mbp_djvu.txt

Brown, D. P., & Fromm, E. (1986). *Hypnotherapy and hypnoanalysis.* Hillsdale, N.J: Lawrence Erlbaum.

Elman, D. (1984). *Hypnotherapy.* Glendale, CA: Westwood.

Fricker, J., & Butler, J. (2000). *Secrets of hypnosis.* New York, NY: DK Kindersley.

Freud, S. (2001). The ego and the id. In J. Strachey (Ed. & Trans.), *The standard edition of the complete psychological works of Sigmund Freud.* (Vol. 19, pp, 13-63). London: Hogarth Press and the Institute of Psycho-Analysis. (Original work published 1923).

Jampolsky, G. (1989). *Out of darkness into the light: A journey of inner healing.* New York, N.Y: Bantom Books.

Kahn, M. (2002). *Basic Freud: Psychoanalytic thought for the 21st century.* New York, N.Y: Basic Books.

Kardiner, A. Foreword. In L. R. Wolfberg's *Hypnoanalysis* (pp. ix-xi). New York, N.Y: Grune & Stratton.

Lindner, R. (1944). *Rebel without a cause: The hypnoanalysis of a criminal psychopath.* New York, N.Y: Grune & Stratton.

Lundholm, J. (2007). *Hypnosis: The experience.* Retrieved from http://www.helium.com/items/158395-hypnosis-the-experience

Lundholm, J. (2013). *A new definition of hypnosis.* Retrieved from http://www.selfgrowth.com/articles/A_New_Definition_of_Hypnosis.html

Murphy, J. (2000). *Power of your subconscious mind.* New York, N.Y: Reward Books.

Quinodoz, J. M. (2004). *Reading Freud: A chronological exploration of Freud's writings: Vol. 1. The New Library of Psychoanalysis Teaching Series* (D. Alcorn, Trans.). New York, N.Y: Routledge.

Sadock, B. J. (1998). *Synopsis of psychiatry: Behavioral sciences/clinical psychiatry* (9th ed.). New York, NY: Lippincott Williams & Wilkins.

Sigmund Freud: Conflict and culture. (2010). *Section II: The individual: Therapy and theory.* Retrieved from The Library of Congress http://www.loc.gov/exhibits/freud/freud02.html

Strachey, J. (Ed. & Trans.). (2001). Papers on hypnotism and suggestion: Editor's introduction. In J. Strachey & A. Freud (Eds.), *The standard edition of the complete psychological works of Sigmund Freud: Vol. 1 (1886-1899). Pre-psycho-analytic publications and unpublished drafts* (pp. 63-69). (Original work published 1920).

VandenBos, G. R. (Ed.). (2007). *American Psychological Association's dictionary of psychology.* Washington, D.C: APA.

Wolfberg, L. R. (1945). *Hypnoanalysis.* New York, N.Y: Grune & Stratton.